AMERICAN JAGUAR

BIG CATS,
BIOGEOGRAPHY,
AND
HUMAN BORDERS

ELIZABETH WEBB

TWENTY-FIRST CENTURY BOOKS / MINNEAPOLIS

Twenty-First Century Books™
An imprint of Lerner Publishing Group, Inc.
241 First Avenue North
Minneapolis, MN 55401 USA

For reading levels and more information, look up this title at www.lernerbooks.com.

Main body text set in Adobe Garamond Pro.
Typeface provided by Adobe Systems.

Library of Congress Cataloging-in-Publication Data

Names: Webb, Elizabeth, 1966– author.
Title: American jaguar : big cats, biogeography, and human borders / Elizabeth Webb.
Description: Minneapolis : Twenty-First Century Books, [2020] | Audience: Ages 13–18. |
    Audience: Grades 9–12. | Includes bibliographical references and index. |
Identifiers: LCCN 2018040958 (print) | LCCN 2019000456 (ebook) |
    ISBN 9781541562684 (eb pdf) | ISBN 9781541523678 (lb : alk. paper)
Subjects: LCSH: Jaguar—Effect of human beings on—Mexican-American Border
    Region—Juvenile literature. | Jaguar—Conservation—Mexican-American Border
    Region—Juvenile literature.
Classification: LCC QL737.C23 (ebook) | LCC QL737.C23 L677 2020 (print) | DDC
    333.95/9755—dc23

LC record available at https://lccn.loc.gov/2018040958

Manufactured in the United States of America
1-44491-34699-3/11/2021

TABLE OF CONTENTS

WELCOME TO THE BORDERLANDS

One cold and windy day late in the winter of 1996, near his ranch in the Peloncillo Mountains along the United States–Mexico border, rancher Warner Glenn was on the trail of a mountain lion.

For Glenn, it was the fourth day of a long and grueling hunt, even for a fourth-generation rancher who had spent decades in these lands. For hours the hunter and his hounds stalked the cat through the jagged mountain landscape. Glenn followed on horseback while his dogs moved ahead, rifling through the underbrush, sniffing out rocks and crags, trying desperately to keep on the trail of the elusive and dangerous cat. During the chase, Glenn was astonished by the speed and distance the cat covered across the mountain ridges. It seemed always to be just out of reach, never close enough to get a look, let alone a good shot with his rifle. Occasionally, Glenn spotted unusual tracks. They didn't look like mountain lion tracks.

Finally, after hours and miles of the chase across the mountain ridges and valleys, Glenn and his team of dogs finally caught up to the cat. There, on a bluff high above the desert, the animal stood on a rocky ledge and looked back at its pursuers. But it wasn't a grizzled mountain lion. Instead, Glenn found himself staring at a magnificent, spotted jaguar.

A seasoned cat hunter like Glenn knew the prize he had stumbled upon. No one had seen a jaguar in the United States for decades. This would be the ultimate trophy for any big-game hunter. But instead of raising his rifle,

Glenn took out his camera. He began snapping photos of the big cat. Glenn's images would become the first photographs of a living wild jaguar in the United States.

The chase soon resumed, and the hunter and his hounds followed the big cat through the mountains. Occasionally, the dogs got too close and the massive beast would hold its ground, spitting and swiping at the pursuing hounds. Glenn wanted to get closer but grew concerned for his dogs. One swing from a frightened and cornered jaguar could easily kill a small dog.

After several hours of pursuit—and a host of remarkable photos—Glenn and his dogs eventually lost the cat's trail. The chase was over as quickly as it began. The jaguar vanished back into the wilds.

Days later, Glenn's photos made the local papers. It wasn't long before his encounter with a jaguar made national headlines too. Over the next few years, several other jaguars would be seen roaming the Borderlands. The jaguar had returned to the United States.

Since Warner Glenn's groundbreaking photos were taken, scientists have installed cameras around the US-Mexico border to capture more images of jaguars.

In the Borderlands between the United States and Mexico, the jaguar is fighting to regain its natural habitat. Some say the jaguar has made a triumphant return to the United States. Others say the jaguar never left—the big cat was here all along, hiding in the most remote areas of the Borderlands.

In the twenty-first century, the jaguar lives in a changing world. Fences, roads, cities, and towns divide the cat's realm. Copper mines and farmland further cut up its natural habitat. Even with all these changes, the jaguar still faces its greatest challenge yet: the border wall between the United States and Mexico, should it ever be completed, will ensure the big cat never steps foot in the United States again.

Habitat fragmentation, or breaking up an animal's vast territory into smaller unconnected sections, threatens many wild animals. In fact, it might be the biggest threat to all wildlife across the globe. The jaguar is not alone in suffering from the effects of all these changes to the land through habitat fragmentation. The pronghorn antelope and bighorn sheep, as well as the diamondback rattlesnake, the burrowing owl, the spadefoot toad, the monarch butterfly, and countless others are all at risk. Border walls, highways, and other human barriers prevent all of these species from moving freely across their natural landscapes to find food, water, shelter, and mates, directly affecting their populations. Climate change threatens to push many species even further toward the brink. To adapt to changes in temperature and the ecological changes that follow, animals must be able to move freely and without obstacles to areas where they can survive. Scientists and citizens alike are working hard to reconnect landscapes in the Borderlands and beyond. Connections across landscapes—and across human borders—are more important than ever. For some creatures, their very future may depend on it.

CHAPTER 1

RULER OF THE SKY ISLANDS

The Sierra Madre Occidental, or "mother mountains to the west," is an immense mountain range that forms the backbone of western Mexico. This towering range starts in the tropical lands of southern Mexico and runs about 780 miles (1,250 km) north to the arid, dry deserts in the state of Sonora, which borders the United States. Here, the mountain range begins to split apart into isolated peaks separated by rolling grasslands and desert. These are the Sky Islands, a loose network of about sixty small mountain ranges. The Sky Islands sprawl northward into the United States in southeastern Arizona.

The Sky Islands provide high-altitude habitats for animals to escape the suffocating heat on the desert floor, where summer temperatures can easily exceed 115 F (46 C). Some of these Sky Island peaks reach almost 12,000 feet (3,657 m) above sea level. At this altitude, the mountains are covered in lush forests of oak and pine and are often snowcapped in the winter months.

The mountains that make up the Sky Islands near and along the US-Mexico border are so tall that, when spotted at a distance, they often appear to be floating above the clouds. These mountains are host to some unique habitats and a huge variety of plant and animal species.

These mountain peaks are among the most biodiverse landscapes in the entire world. Here, two worlds collide. Plants and animals associated with cooler, temperate northern climates live alongside those from warmer, tropical southern climates. Desert plants such as cactus and agave blend in with palm trees, oaks, and pines. Bears, parrots, deer, and eagles all call the Sky Islands home. So does an unusual mix of cats, including the jaguar and its tiny spotted cousin, the ocelot (*Leopardus pardalis*), which typically live in tropical areas of Central and South America. Meanwhile, the mountain lion (*Puma concolor*) and bobcat (*Lynx rufus*) are associated with cooler regions such as the Rocky Mountains of the western United States. Yet here in the Sky Islands, all of these cats live side by side.

For thousands of years, the jaguar has claimed the Sky Islands as its home. But it wasn't always like that. The jaguar had to earn its role as top cat.

EVOLUTION OF A BIG CAT

All cats are members of the taxonomic family Felidae. Scientists recognize thirty-seven species of felids from around the world, ranging from leopards and lions (*Panthera leo*) to mountain lions, bobcats, and the average house cat (*Felis catus*). All of these modern cats are descendants of one ancient and enormous felid, *Pseudaelurus*, which lived in Europe and Asia about twenty million years ago.

THE NAME GAME

Earth is full of billions of different kinds of living things, or organisms. Throughout history, to make it easier to study and talk about these living things, scientists have developed ways to organize and categorize organisms. The science of naming, describing, and classifying living things is taxonomy. Scientists study the behavior, anatomy, and other characteristics of living things to separate them into groups of related creatures. This type of classification also helps with understanding evolutionary relationships. The broadest category of living things is the domain. The three domains are Archaea, Bacteria, and Eukarya. From there, organisms are broken down into narrower categories: kingdom, phylum, class, order, family, genus, and species. Organisms of the same species are able to mate and produce viable offspring.

In the eighteenth century, Swedish botanist Carl Linnaeus invented a consistent and efficient system for naming individual organisms. He chose Latin as the main language of taxonomy. A specific genus and species name refers to one organism. For example, the scientific name for the jaguar is *Panthera onca*. The two-word taxonomic naming system is known as binomial nomenclature. Although few people speak or use the language, Latin acts as a universal language of science. The jaguar's taxonomic classification is as follows:

Eukarya (domain)
Animalia (kingdom)
Chordata (phylum)
Mammalia (class)
Carnivora (order)
Felidae (family)
Panthera (genus)
P. onca (species)

During the first few million years of *Pseudaelurus*'s reign, sea levels fell considerably, exposing land between the continents of Asia and Africa and between Asia and North America. Early humans and other animals moved across the exposed lands, known as land bridges, to settle in other regions. In North America, early felids crossed the Bering Land Bridge, which connected what is now eastern Russia to Alaska. As the first descendants of *Pseudaelurus* adapted to their new homes, they developed new and different traits for survival. Eventually, different species of cats evolved as the environment changed. One of

THE BIG CATS

Scientists view all species of the genus *Panthera* as the big cats. In the twenty-first century, the jaguar is the only member of this genus in the Americas. *Panthera* also includes the large cats of Africa—lions and leopards—as well as the tigers of Asia. *Panthera* is the oldest of cat lineages, or descendants. It first appeared in the fossil record about 10.8 million years ago.

Besides being really big, all big cats can roar. All mammals, including cats, have a larynx, an organ in the neck that helps produce sound. (In humans, we call it a voice box.) The larynx is made up of many muscles, ligaments, and small bones. One important bone that allows the larynx to make sounds is the hyoid bone.

All members of *Panthera* have a hyoid bone that is not entirely ossified, or hardened. The hyoid bone in a big cat is a series of small bones that are connected with ligaments and other tissues. This allows the hyoid bone to be very flexible. When air is forced over the hyoid, the bone reverberates to make a deep, thunderous vocalization, or a roar.

Scientists view all other species of cats as small cats. These include ocelots, bobcats, lynxes, and domestic cats. Even the these was *Panthera*, a group of big cats that would eventually become what we recognize in the twenty-first century as lions, tigers, leopards, and jaguars.

AGE OF GIANT BEASTS

Modern-day jaguars are remnants from the Pleistocene epoch, a geologic period from 2.5 million to 13,000 years ago. During the Pleistocene epoch, North America was dominated by huge mammals such as mammoths and mastodons (creatures that share the same

African cheetah and mighty mountain lion are just oversized small cats. In these small cats, the hyoid bone is ossified and doesn't have the elasticity (flexibility) that helps produce a roar. However, the small cats' fully ossified hyoid bone allows them to do something that their big *Panthera* cousins cannot do: purr.

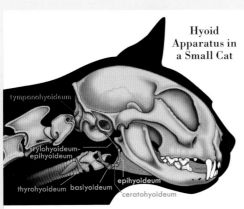

Hyoid Apparatus in a Small Cat

tympanohyoideum

stylohyoideum-epihyoideum

thyrohyoideum basiyoideum

epihyoideum

ceratohyoideum

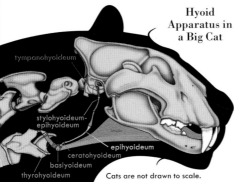

Hyoid Apparatus in a Big Cat

tympanohyoideum

stylohyoideum-epihyoideum

epihyoideum

ceratohyoideum

basiyoideum

thyrohyoideum

Cats are not drawn to scale.

Depending on the species, cats have differently structured hyoid bones. The bones affect the cats' vocalizations. Those with open hyoid bones can roar, while those with closed ones can purr. This skeletal difference distinguishes the "big cats" from the "small cats."

ancestors as elephants), the short-faced bear, and the giant ground sloth. North America was also home to several species of big cats, including the American lion (*Panthera atrox*), American leopard, and the family of saber-toothed cats known as *Smilodon*. It was also home to the ancestor of the modern jaguar.

While the jaguar was only one of several large cats wandering North America, the competition was about to get very thin. At the end of the Pleistocene epoch, Earth's climate was going

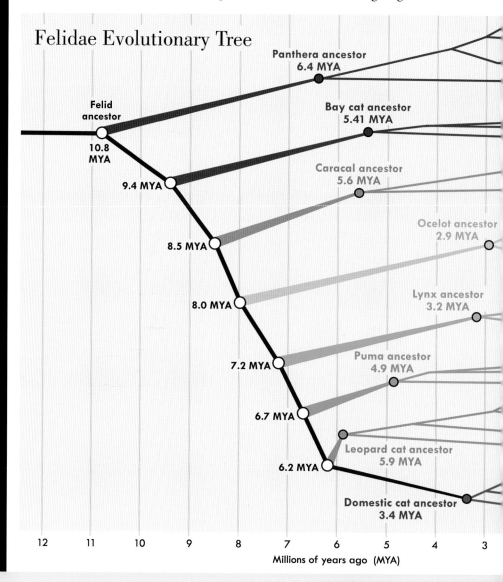

Felidae Evolutionary Tree

Panthera ancestor
6.4 MYA

Felid ancestor
10.8 MYA

Bay cat ancestor
5.41 MYA

9.4 MYA

Caracal ancestor
5.6 MYA

8.5 MYA

Ocelot ancestor
2.9 MYA

8.0 MYA

Lynx ancestor
3.2 MYA

7.2 MYA

Puma ancestor
4.9 MYA

6.7 MYA

Leopard cat ancestor
5.9 MYA

6.2 MYA

Domestic cat ancestor
3.4 MYA

12   11   10   9   8   7   6   5   4   3

Millions of years ago (MYA)

through vast changes. During various ice ages, huge sheets of ice flowed across North America, carving out lake and river basins and scouring the landscape to create vast plains. Earth cooled considerably, and the thick tropical jungles that had once covered North America faded away, replaced by temperate forests, plains, swamps, and deserts.

At about that time, *Homo sapiens* moved into North America, migrating along the same land bridges as earlier mammals. Hunting by these first humans likely contributed to the extinction of the continent's largest, slow-moving mammals. A changing climate also impacted the animals' ability to survive. As a result of human hunters and changes in climate and the environment, nearly 75 percent of all large mammals in North America died out. One by one, all the ancient

Lion *Panthera leo*
Leopard *Panthera pardus*
Jaguar *Panthera onca*
Tiger *Panthera tigris*
Snow leopard *Panthera uncia*
Clouded leopard *Neofelis nebulosa*
Bornean clouded leopard *Neofelis diardi*

Asian golden cat *Pardofelis temminckii*
Bornean bay cat *Pardofelis badia*
Marbled cat *Pardofelis marmorata*

Caracal *Caracal caracal*
African golden cat *Caracal aurata*
Serval *Leptailurus serval*

Geoffroy's cat *Leopardus geoffroyi*
Kodkod *Leopardus guigna*
Oncilla *Leopardus tigrinus*
Andean mountain cat *Leopardus jacobita*
Pampas cat *Leopardus colocolo*
Margay *Leopardus wiedii*
Ocelot *Leopardus pardalis*

Iberian lynx *Lynx pardinus*
Eurasian lynx *Lynx lynx*
Canada lynx *Lynx canadensis*
Bobcat *Lynx rufus*

Puma *Puma concolor*
Jaguarundi *Puma yagouaroundi*
Cheetah *Acinonyx jubatus*

Asian leopard cat *Prionailurus bengalensis*
Fishing cat *Prionailurus viverrinus*
Flat-headed cat *Prionailurus planiceps*
Rusty-spotted cat *Prionailurus rubiginosus*
Pallas's cat *Otocolobus manul*

Domestic cat *Felis catus*
Wildcat *Felis silvestris*
Sand cat *Felis margarita*
Black-footed cat *Felis nigripes*
Jungle cat *Felis chaus*

This diagram shows how all species of cats descend from a common ancestor, which existed some eleven million years ago. This common ancestor gradually evolved into several different species, including the common ancestor of lions, tigers, and jaguars. Although this diagram excludes some species and subspecies, biologists believe this to be an accurate depiction of the evolution of all known felines.

1   Today

big cats disappeared from the Americas. By the end of the Pleistocene, the jaguar was the only surviving species of *Panthera* in the Western Hemisphere. Freed from competition, the jaguar became the top cat of the Americas.

THE JAGUAR'S RANGE

The Holocene epoch that followed the Pleistocene is the current geological era. By the beginning of the Holocene, almost all giant mammals that had once dominated the North American landscape were extinct. Smaller-bodied animals were more adapted to the cooler and more variable climate, and prey species such as tapir (a piglike animal) and deer evolved into smaller forms in response to these environmental changes. The jaguar also evolved into small forms. Modern-day jaguars are considerably smaller than the larger Pleistocene ones.

These changes also influenced evolution of other cat species in North America. The mountain lion and lynx adapted to the cooler, temperate (mild) climates of North America, whereas the jaguar claimed the lush, tropical lands of what are now Central and South America as its home. Still, this didn't prevent the cat from extending its range northward into what would become the United States. Jaguar remains have been found as far north as Washington State and as far east as Pennsylvania and Florida.

The jaguar's range still includes many different ecosystems. Jaguars are found in deserts, jungles, and swamps from the US-Mexico Borderlands, through coastal Central America, and deep into South America. Some of these big cats have even been found wandering the beaches of Central America.

Just how many jaguars live in the wild varies greatly depending on the source. Some conservation groups estimate the range-wide population of jaguars to be only about fifteen thousand individuals. However, a recent study suggested that the global population is more like 173,000. Regardless, all experts agree that global jaguar populations are steadily declining.

In the Borderlands of Arizona, the cat tends to stay in the mountains of the Sky Islands where cooler temperatures prevail. In the Sky Islands of northern Mexico the cat has found a home in foothills thornscrub, a unique habitat of steep and secluded canyons where short and dense subtropical vegetation such as acacia and cacti mixes with grasslands and oak woodlands. Thornscrub is an unwelcoming habitat for humans, so it is perfect for a secretive and elusive predator like a big cat.

THE PERFECT PREDATOR

Jaguar size varies depending on its available prey. The jaguar's northern range is in the desert mountains of Sonora, Mexico, and the Sky Islands of Arizona, which have fewer species of prey animals. Jaguars from the lush jungles of South America have a much larger prey base and variety of prey animals to eat. A male jaguar from the Borderlands region might weigh only 120 pounds (54 kg). But a well-fed male jaguar in South America can weigh up to 350 pounds (159 kg)!

Regardless of where it roams, the jaguar is unique among predators in the Americas because of its power and strength. Unlike its lanky cousin, the mountain lion, jaguars are stocky and compact. They also possess remarkable muscle density, so they are extremely strong for their size. The jaguar's skeletal structure also contributes to its power. The big cat has a short and stout jawbone with few teeth, allowing more room for large jaw muscles. So the jaguar has the most powerful bite of all the big cats. While many other cats prefer to subdue larger prey by biting and holding the windpipe to suffocate their meal, the jaguar relies on overwhelming force. The cat is known to easily snap bones with one bite and to puncture its prey's skull with its teeth to kill it instantly.

Jaguars have specialized teeth. Their canines, the large and sharp fangs near the front of the skull, are highly sensitive. Lined with nerve endings, these teeth allow the cat to quickly locate soft tissue, usually along the prey's neck. The jaguar's deadly canines sink into the soft flesh, cutting flesh between vertebrae (bones in the spine). The prey's spinal column is severed instantly, paralyzing the animal before it meets a gruesome death.

Like all other wild cats, jaguars hunt at night. Aiding this hunting behavior is a thin membrane in their eyes, a *tapetum lucidum*. This membrane helps concentrate all available light to the optic nerve in the eye that processes images. This allows the cat to see better under low-light conditions. This membrane is responsible for eyeshine in cats.

A jaguar's bite delivers a force of about 1,500 pounds per square inch (105 kg per sq. cm), about a third of the strength of a saltwater crocodile's bite. With such a powerful jaw, jaguars can easily drag their prey out of rivers and up trees.

ROSETTES

The spotted patterns on a jaguar's coat are rosettes. Every jaguar's coat bears a unique set of rosettes, not unlike human fingerprints. Researchers can identify individual jaguars by these unique patterns. Being able to distinguish among individual jaguars is critical for understanding how many jaguars live within an area and how long they survive.

For the jaguar, rosettes play a much more important role. These fur patterns most likely allow the cat to blend into the surroundings where it stalks its prey. The busy patterns can help confuse prey species—even briefly. This is especially effective in the low-light conditions the jaguar prefers for hunting. For prey being stalked in the thick underbrush, just a moment's hesitation can be the difference between life and death.

Over the years, the jaguar has also paid a price for its beautiful coat. Throughout its range, hunters still pursue the jaguar for its fur. Poaching (illegal hunting) is still a serious problem in Central and South America, where a jaguar pelt can be worth a small fortune on the black market, where illegal goods are bought and sold.

PREY

For such a wide-ranging predator, the jaguar tends to stick to a few staples in its diet. Nearly 98 percent of its prey is other warm-blooded mammals, including deer, as well as tapirs and peccaries (javelinas), piglike mammals found in Central and South America. Depending on where the jaguar roams, other common prey animals can include anteaters, armadillos, and even monkeys. The remaining portion of their diet might include local, cold-blooded reptiles such as turtles, iguanas, or caimans (small South American crocodiles).

You might not expect it, but jaguars are water-loving cats. Unlike most other wild cats, jaguars don't consider rivers and lakes as barriers and regularly swim across waterways. The big cat is also quite good at catching fish.

BLACK PANTHER

One famous member of the *Panthera* genus is the black panther. A black panther is not a separate species of *Panthera*. A black panther is a jaguar or leopard that is melanistic—its skin and fur have an abundance of melanin, or dark pigment, making its coat appear black. In the Americas, most black panthers are melanistic jaguars. In Africa black panthers are melanistic leopards, the closest relative of the jaguar and another big cat with a spotted fur pattern. If you look closely at that dark coat of the black panther, you can still see some of the rosette and spotted patterns common to other jaguars and leopards.

As jaguars prowl through forest and desert terrains, their powerful muscles move smoothly under their spotted pelts. Those lucky enough to see a jaguar in person can agree that jaguar pelts are most beautiful on a living, breathing jaguar.

Jaguars usually live alone and travel great distances in search of food. Like most predators, the jaguar is an opportunistic hunter, taking a meal where it can find one. Every once in a while, that might mean a stinky meal. Jaguars are known to eat the various skunks found throughout the Americas. One jaguar in South America was even found with a stomach full of frogs.

The big cat's favorite method for capturing prey is to stalk and ambush, relying on a combination of surprise and overwhelming power. Like all cats, the jaguar is sneaky, using the soft pads of its feet to silently prowl for prey. Whiskers function as feelers to help the cat to navigate dense underbrush. The cat will stalk its prey, silently and patiently, moving as close as possible. The jaguar then uses an explosive burst of speed to quickly pounce. From there, the jaguar uses sheer power to bring down its meal.

Jaguars feed on their kill for a couple of days, alternating between feeding and resting before moving on to stalk more prey. Unlike mountain lions, jaguars don't cover or bury their kill to protect it from other animals while they are resting. Jaguars will stay with their new kill, lingering nearby to scare off any would-be scavengers that might move in on the cat's hard-earned meal.

THE WANDERER

Jaguars are solitary in nature. Adults meet one another only to mate or when two cats accidentally stumble across each other. They can travel great distances in search of food or to protect their territory. Like other cats, jaguars communicate through various means. As they pass through their landscape, jaguars use scent glands in their cheeks. By rubbing against trees or rocks, a jaguar can leave behind its scent, telling other cats about its presence. Marking the ground with their urine is another way the cats communicate with one another in the wild.

Two jaguars rarely come into contact with each other. But when it happens, jaguars tend to avoid conflict, likely because even a scuffle could result in serious, life-threatening injuries. A small bite or scratch could become infected and pose a threat to the cat's survival. Broken claws or damaged eyes could also be a death sentence for a large predator like a jaguar. These injuries can prevent them from effectively finding food or protecting themselves from competition. Communication between big cats is critical in avoiding these confrontations.

Most of the time, jaguars only associate with other individuals for mating. These big cats have no set breeding season and have been known to mate at any time of the year. The cats usually reach breeding age by the age of two or three. About six months after a successful mating, the female gives birth to two to four cubs. Shortly after mating, the male jaguar wanders off, which means the female will raise the cubs alone.

DISPERSAL

All plants and animals eventually leave their natal ranges (the area where they were born). They disperse, or move away, to find their own territory and their own mates. Dispersal happens in a variety of ways, through wind, water, and physical migration. Jaguars sometimes disperse hundreds of miles from their natal range. Small animals, such as salamanders, might disperse only a few hundred meters. Plants disperse with the help of birds, which eat seeds and spread them—sometimes miles away—through their droppings. Through dispersal, animals and plants have a chance to meet, mate, and exchange genetic material.

It's a dangerous world for the young cubs. Although they will grow up to be deadly predators sitting atop the food chain, jaguar cubs spend their first several months as helpless young cubs, hidden away in dens. Mother jaguars also protect their cubs from harm since young jaguars are part of the food chain too. Animals such as coyotes can easily kill jaguar cubs that have been left alone. And another adult jaguar won't hesitate to kill the young of another cat.

As the young cubs grow, they will follow their mother to learn to hunt and survive in a dangerous world. After eighteen to thirty-six months, the young will be ready to leave their mother and strike out to find their own territory. Just how large a territory an adult jaguar requires depends on the available resources. In Guatemala, Belize, and other Central American countries, the jaguar population is relatively dense, with many animals living within a particular area. Here, habitats and resources like food are abundant, so a male jaguar will be able to find what he needs to survive in a small territory of only about 10 square miles (26 sq. km). In the Sky Islands region of the Borderlands, where resources are more limited, male cats need larger territories to find enough food and mates to survive and reproduce. Borderlands jaguars might have home ranges of hundreds of square miles. But females usually have home ranges less than half the size of males. Female jaguars tend to stay in smaller areas since they take care of the cubs, which do not go far from the mother's den until they are grown.

Like all larger cats, male jaguars tend to settle far away from their natal territories, the territories where they were born. Often their mothers chase them away, forcing them to seek out their own territory far away from their natal range. Young male jaguars might travel up to 500 miles (805 km) from where they were born to find their own territory. They may have to compete with older, more dominant males that will fiercely defend space from any newcomers.

For young Borderlands jaguars seeking new territories of their own, the modern world poses serious threats. Animals often have to navigate a complex landscape of man-made barriers such as roads and fences, as well as cities, towns, and farmlands. Competing with other jaguars and predators is one thing. Competing with *Homo sapiens* is something completely different for the top predator of the Borderlands.

CONSERVATION CONNECTION
HOME RANGE AND TERRITORY

A home range is the area where an animal seeks food, mates, and shelter. Individual home ranges can partially overlap. For mating, male and female jaguars have overlapping ranges so they can come in contact with one another. When home ranges of dominant males overlap, however, it can sometimes lead to conflict. A territory is a smaller area within a home range. Territories do not overlap, and jaguars often fiercely defend their own territory.

CHAPTER 2

THE ALL-AMERICAN CAT

Jaguars have had a long and complex relationship with humans. Both species were often in direct competition for food. Occasionally, humans even found themselves on the menu for large predators like jaguars.

In North America, humans have probably been interacting with jaguars for more than eleven thousand years. Some humans revered the big cat. They respected its physical prowess, and they understood the jaguar's role in the natural world as an apex, or top, predator.

HE WHO KILLS WITH ONE LEAP

Many ancient civilizations throughout the Americas showed respect for the big cat. In fact, the word *jaguar* comes from *yaguara*, a term used by Indigenous peoples of the Amazon River basin in South America. *Yaguara* loosely translates to "He Who Kills with One Leap."

To the early cultures of Mesoamerica, the region that is modern Mexico and Central America, the jaguar's power and secretive habits elevated the creature to a position of honor and respect. The Olmec were one of the earliest of Mesoamerican civilizations to thrive in what would become southern Mexico. They viewed the jaguar as a cave god, one who was responsible for the terrifying earthquakes that sometimes shake this portion of the world. The Olmec vanished around 300 BCE, and the many statues and other artifacts they left behind captured their respect for the jaguar. One common image in Olmec art was the were-jaguar, a half-man, half-jaguar creature.

The Maya people of the Yucatán Peninsula in parts of modern-day Mexico, Guatemala, and Belize, also revered the big cat. To the Maya, the jaguar played an important role in religion as the sun god, Ah Kinchil, who brought light to the world during the day. At night he turned into the Jaguar God and wandered the dark underworld. Many jaguar figures and symbols have been recovered from the Maya city-state of Palenque in southern Mexico. Chichén Itzá, which was the capital of the Mayan Empire, is home to the Temple of the Jaguar. The presence of the jaguar in art and architecture are clear clues the mighty cat played an important role in Maya civilization.

Jaguars were a common symbol in ancient Mesoamerican art, indicating to historians and anthropologists that the animal was culturally significant.

As the Maya civilization declined around 900 CE, the Toltec civilization was growing. Symbolism of the jaguar played a role in Toltec culture too. The image of the fierce and bold cat, along with that of the eagle, became important symbols for the Toltec military. The Aztecs, who eventually conquered the Toltec in 1168 CE, viewed the jaguar as the bravest of all beasts. So they named the band of warriors who protected the glorious capital of Tenochtitlán, in what would eventually become Mexico City, the Jaguar Knights.

Jaguar imagery also shows up in some of the ancient cultures of the North American Southwest. Ancestors of groups such as the Pueblo and Hopi, who resided in what has become Arizona and New Mexico, left behind some jaguar imagery in paintings, artwork, and other artifacts.

ONZA, THE LEGENDARY BEAST OF THE BORDERLANDS

Legend has it that Bigfoot roams the forests of the Pacific Northwest. The Loch Ness Monster is said to inhabit a lake in Scotland. The Borderlands has its own legendary creature too. Legends of rural Mexico describe the *onza* as the offspring of a male jaguar and a female mountain lion. The cat is said to have a broad chest, lean legs, and a dark coat with a pale underside. Its yellow eyes glow like fire in the night. The *onza* preys on dogs, its mortal enemy, and is said to hunt young people who stray from their homes at night. Some stories claim the creature has supernatural powers like those of a witch.

By the twentieth century, legends of the *onza* had crossed the border into the United States. Several American adventurers traveled to northern Mexico to find the mysterious *onza*. A pair of US government-sponsored expeditions gathered in-depth records of the wildlife of Mexico, from birds to reptiles and mammals (including big cats). None of these efforts uncovered fact-based evidence of the mythic *onza*. Yet the legend of the *onza* is still alive in rural parts of northern Mexico.

JAGUAR AND THE AMERICAN WEST

The reverence and respect for the jaguar, as well as other large predators, faded away as Europeans began to settle the Americas. Unlike Indigenous peoples, many of whom revered the natural world as a spiritual force and precious resource, Europeans instead practiced a philosophy of conquest. By the 1800s, ranching and farming transformed the wild landscape of the American West. As cattle ranching became a big business, large sections of the lands where wild animals such as buffalo, wolves, and big cats once roamed were fenced off. Then railroads and gold fever took more settlers farther west, and large predators were quickly displaced. Ranchers viewed large predators as a threat to humans and cattle alike, so they hunted, poisoned, or simply chased them off their lands. Federal and local governments, through the Department of Agriculture, offered bounties, or cash rewards, for the carcasses of large predators such as coyotes, wolves, mountain lions, and jaguars. County records from 1913 in Texas, for example, show that hunters earned $5 for every jaguar, mountain lion, and wolf killed, while coyotes and bobcats earned hunters only $1 each. (That's currently about $129 and $26, respectively.) During the early 1900s, professional hunters flocked to the Southwest to earn a living from these bounties.

The bounty business flourished, but with their stealth and secretive ways, jaguars managed to hang on—though in very low numbers—in the wildest, most rugged landscapes of the American Southwest. By the twentieth century, the jaguar was nearly eliminated from the United States.

THE AGE OF CONSERVATION

At about that time, the public perception of wildlife and wild areas was beginning to change in the United States. The conservation movement had begun in the late 1800s as a reaction to rapid settlement of the American West. Championing the beauty of open spaces and the wildlife that lived there, the movement sought to protect natural habitats and creatures.

KEYSTONE SPECIES

A keystone species is a plant or animal that plays a critical role in maintaining the health of an ecosystem. Without it, that ecosystem would change dramatically or cease to exist. For example, the beaver (*Castor canadensis*) is a keystone species. Beavers often build dams along streams or rivers. The dam creates a pond, providing habitats for other plants and animals in that ecosystem. Keystone species can also help maintain healthy populations of living creatures within an ecosystem. Large predators such as wolves, for example, can be a keystone species because they prey on elk, keeping the elk populations in check. Too many elk might overgraze on plants and small trees, decreasing the habitats available to other animals within that ecosystem.

In 1905 conservationist president Theodore Roosevelt established the US Forest Service, a federal agency charged with protecting and managing the vast network of forests in the United States. Years later in 1916, President Woodrow Wilson signed an act creating the National Park Service. Although Yellowstone and Yosemite National Parks had existed for decades, Wilson's new legislation would create a vast network of parks aimed at protecting the nation's unique natural heritage. The National Park System became a worldwide model for the conservation of wildlife and wildlands.

By the early 1900s, even as the conservation movement gained popularity, hunting and fishing were still largely unregulated. Wildlife populations among deer, elk (*Cervus canadensis*), and bighorn sheep (*Ovis canadensis*) began to plummet thanks to unregulated hunting. Game birds such as ducks and turkeys had serious population declines too. Fashion trends of the nineteenth and early twentieth centuries demanded bird feathers for women's hats. Many bird species, such as egrets, were illegally killed for their feathers across the United States and in other parts of the world. Outdoor enthusiasts began to notice. Something needed to be done.

The next few decades witnessed a series of groundbreaking laws that conserved wildlife and natural habitats. By 1913, some states had begun to require hunters to purchase hunting licenses to regulate the number of animals that humans could lawfully kill. The Migratory Bird Treaty Act, passed by the US Congress in 1918, protected nearly all species of birds from needless killing. In 1937 Congress passed the Pittman-Robertson Act. This groundbreaking law required that any tax money collected from the sales of firearms and ammunition, whether for hunting or other purposes, get redistributed to states to fund wildlife conservation projects, habitat restoration, and wildlife research.

With conservation efforts and wildlife management, bounty programs aimed at thinning predator populations soon came to an end. Local communities, states, and the US government made sure that laws and other regulations helped maintain wild animal populations. This conservation philosophy became known as wildlife management. For the first time in US history, it was more profitable to manage large predator species than it was to kill them for bounty programs. Wildlife management would help protect wildlife and their habitats for future generations.

CONSERVATION CONNECTION
WILDLIFE MANAGEMENT

Wildlife management is actively monitoring and controlling animal and plant populations so they remain healthy and sustainable. Scientists and lawmakers work together in wildlife management. For example, states keep counts of deer and trout populations. Each year, based on scientists' recommendations, the states with these species establish quotas, or limits, for how many deer can be legally hunted and how many fish may be legally caught. Other forms of wildlife management protect the habitat of an endangered bird species or remove an invasive plant that is taking over an area and forcing out local species.

ALDO LEOPOLD, THE FATHER OF WILDLIFE CONSERVATION

Aldo Leopold examines specimens of birds.

Aldo Leopold was a scientist, writer, hunter, and naturalist. Conservationists point to him as the father of the wilderness movement and the most influential person in shaping Americans' relationship with wildlife and wild places. Born in Iowa in 1887, Leopold developed many of his ideas as a young man working for the US Forest Service in Arizona and New Mexico. Leopold led an effort to establish the Gila National Forest in New Mexico. In 1924 Gila became the first of 765 protected wilderness areas in the United States. These wilderness areas protect sensitive landscapes from development while still allowing the public to visit some of the nation's wildest places.

Leopold believed society had a moral responsibility to care for the natural world. Later, as a professor at the University of Wisconsin—Madison, he championed the idea of a land ethic. This philosophy calls for the responsible management and protection of wildlife, forests, water, and land so they will be around for future generations to enjoy.

Leopold died in 1948, leaving behind an incredible legacy. A collection of his essays, *A Sand County Almanac*, was published shortly after his death. Many view the book as a classic and a must-read for wildlife conservationists. The Aldo Leopold Foundation, based in Baraboo, Wisconsin, carries on his conservation ethic through historic preservation, stewardship of lands, and community education.

CONFLICT

With all these challenges, the jaguar persisted in states like Arizona and New Mexico, although in very small numbers. Relying on its stealth and secretive habits, the jaguar retreated to the wildest, most rugged lands of the American West. Although jaguar bounty programs had ended, the killing of jaguars was still allowed for other reasons, just not for profit. If the animal proved to be a nuisance—by killing or threatening property, people, or livestock—it could be legally killed, no matter what the species. The jaguar's natural tendencies as a large predator would continue to lead to conflicts with humans.

Known as a prey base, the population of native prey animals—such as deer or peccaries—provide jaguars with all the food they need. However, when humans overhunt a jaguar's habitat or when ranchland peccaries and farms take over wild open spaces, the natural prey base can decline sharply. Prey like deer or peccaries either die off or move away. Then jaguars and other large predators have a harder time surviving.

Quite contrary to the stereotypes about cats, jaguars love water and will hunt water-dwelling prey such as caiman.

The jaguar might respond to a declining prey base within its territory by turning to the next available food source. Sometimes this will be cattle, goats, or other livestock. Cattle ranching is important to the economic well-being of the southwestern United States and northern Mexico. When jaguars turn to livestock, the big cats' survival comes in direct conflict with the ranching business. This conflict tends to not end well for the jaguar.

In Mexico, ranchers had hunted jaguars so extensively that the animal's survival was at risk. So the government banned jaguar hunting nationwide in 1987. However, these protections haven't changed the attitudes of ranching communities, which generally view jaguars and mountain lions as threats to their livelihood. Cats in Mexico that threaten livestock are often killed by professional hunters, or *cazadores*, hired by ranchers. These hunts remain probably the greatest threat to jaguars in the Borderlands. One study involving landowners in northern Mexico found that between 1997 and 2000, professional hunters killed at least eleven jaguars because they were perceived as threats to local ranchers. Conservationists suspect that the number of jaguars killed may be much higher since these killings often go unreported. For the jaguars of the Borderlands—where numbers are extremely low already—predator control kills such as these can be devastating to the population of big cats.

RETURN OF THE JAGUAR?

As an apex predator, the jaguar naturally exists in low numbers, whether that's in the dense jungles of South America or in the Borderlands at the northernmost reaches of its range. Animals within any species at the top of a food chain are always much fewer than the number of animals that are lower on that food chain. So such apex predators are especially vulnerable to human influence.

Hunting records can sometimes demonstrate the size of a certain population. These records suggest a steep decline of jaguars in the

United States throughout the twentieth century. From 1900 to 1950, humans killed more than fifty jaguars in Arizona and New Mexico. The animals were hunted, trapped for sport, or killed as part of predator control. In the next fifty years, the number of cats killed plummeted, suggesting that only a small handful of the big cats were occasionally roaming north of the border. While people still occasionally spot male jaguars in the Borderlands, the last known wild female jaguar in the United States was killed by a hunter in 1963.

Over the next several decades only a handful of jaguar sightings were reported in this part of the world. The Borderlands jaguar seemed to be fading into history, just another thing lost from a wilder era—

THE ENDANGERED SPECIES ACT

Passed by the US Congress in 1973 and signed into law by President Richard Nixon, the Endangered Species Act is a series of laws that give widespread protections to plants and animals that scientists believe are at risk of extinction. The US Fish and Wildlife Service (USFWS) and the National Marine Fisheries Service carry out the work, following the guidelines laid out by the act. Scientists do rigorous studies to assess population numbers and threats to a wide variety of plants and animals. These studies determine whether a species is imperiled. Species are then listed as either "endangered," "threatened," or "candidate." Endangered species are those in danger of going extinct. Threatened species are those at risk of being classified as endangered in the near future should their populations decrease. Candidate species are those that scientists are considering for listing as either threatened or endangered, but research is still ongoing.

Once a species is listed as threatened or endangered, the Endangered Species Act provides a wide variety of protections to that species and its habitats. These protections are aimed at before railroads, subdivisions, and barbed wire for cattle—when large predators roamed freely. The jaguars that people reported seeing mostly turned out to be a misidentified mountain lion or bobcat. By the 1990s, it seemed, the American jaguar had faded into legend.

But in 1996, everything changed. Warner Glenn's harrowing tale and breathtaking photographs of his jaguar encounter in the Peloncillo Mountains of Arizona captivated the public. Then, less than six months later, another veteran hunter, Jack Childs, took photos of another jaguar in the mountains right outside of Tucson, Arizona.

The news of these two big cat sightings turned into a national sensation. Jaguars had returned to the United States.

reducing threats, such as habitat loss or overhunting. The USFWS also creates a species-specific recovery plan that outlines the actions required to help save the species from extinction.

A species comes off the list in one of two ways. It goes extinct, or less likely, it recovers. The peregrine falcon (*Falco peregrinus*) and bald eagle (*Haliaeetus leucocephalus*) are two birds of prey that were dangerously close to extinction in the 1970s because of habitat loss, overhunting, and pollution. Both species were listed as endangered not long after the Endangered Species Act came into effect. These listings came with increased protections and programs that reintroduced each species to areas where they had vanished. Following a public outcry, new laws banned certain harmful pollutants, such as DDT (dichlorodiphenyltrichloroethane), a toxic chemical once commonly used in insecticide in the US.

These efforts worked, thanks in large part to the Endangered Species Act. In 1999 the peregrine was delisted, followed by the bald eagle in 2007. The peregrine falcon and bald eagle are once again widespread across North America, a testament to the success of conservation efforts.

NEVER LEFT

With these sightings, interest in jaguar conservation exploded in the United States. State wildlife agencies in Arizona, New Mexico, and across the border in Mexico began working together to protect the jaguar. Massive public outcry to help protect the magnificent cat led to further action. In 1997, less than a year after Glenn snapped his photos, the USFWS finally listed the jaguar as "endangered" under the Endangered Species Act of 1973. This listing gave the cat and its habitats widespread protections throughout its range.

Efforts to look for the cat greatly increased in the Borderlands and beyond. Counting any animal's population numbers is part of ensuring its survival. Since Glenn's 1996 encounter, more than a dozen jaguars have been detected in Arizona and New Mexico. In 2017 alone, three different jaguars were captured on remote wildlife camera traps in distant areas of southern Arizona.

However, even for those very few jaguars that freely roam the Borderlands, life continues to be perilous, and a reminder of a long and complicated history with humans. In the spring of 2018, a jaguar pelt was found at a ranch in Sonora just south of the border. The cat was most likely illegally captured and killed. The male jaguar was known to researchers as Yo'oko and had been captured by camera traps during the previous two years. The loss was a devastating blow to Borderlands jaguars. By 2019 only one other jaguar was known to be roaming the lands north of the US-Mexico border.

HOW TO BUILD A WALL

Even in the face of these challenges, the jaguar is a survivor. It has endured historical mass extinctions and outlasted other ancient cats that couldn't adapt. It has been worshipped gloriously in Mesoamerican culture, and it has been hunted to near-extinction in the modern Americas. Still, for the jaguars of the Borderlands, nothing could prepare it for the threats of the twenty-first century—

habitat fragmentation as a result of a border wall between the United States and Mexico. The mighty jaguar was about to face its toughest foe yet.

The 2,000-mile (3,218 km) border between the United States and Mexico is at the center of a political firestorm. Caught in the middle of the dispute are the wild animals and landscapes that call both nations home.

Existing sections of the border "wall" take many different forms. In areas where the border crosses mountains or rivers, the wall might be a barbed-wire fence. Sometimes it's a vehicle barrier, a long row of giant iron *X*s that cuts through the desert to prevent trucks and cars from crossing the border in remote areas. However, along many hundreds of miles of the border, the wall is a pedestrian fence, a massive iron wall impassible for people—and most wildlife.

In recent decades, the US government has added miles and miles of additional pedestrian fencing to the US-Mexico border. Following the attacks of September 11, 2001, during the peak of hysteria about terrorists, immigrants, and drug dealers coming across the southern border, many laws intended to protect the environment, Native American heritage, and personal property rights

Vehicle barriers still allow most wildlife to move freely across the US-Mexico border.

BORDER WALL BY THE NUMBERS

The United States–Mexico border stretches for **1,954 miles (3,145 km)**.

- **654 miles (1,053 km):** border walls, pedestrian fencing, and vehicle barriers
- **1,300 miles (2,092 km):** no barriers

The Arizona-Mexico border covers **373 miles (600 km)**.

- **123 miles (198 km):** pedestrian fencing
- **183 miles (295 km):** vehicle barriers
- **67 miles (107 km):** no barriers

Nine sectors along the border are covered by **18,600 Border Patrol agents**.

Along the border are **50 official crossing sites**.

The international border between the United States and Mexico has been largely blocked off to prevent people from crossing at sites other than those sanctioned by each country's government. This map shows the locations of different types of barriers. The Rio Grande forms a natural barrier where it runs between Texas and Mexico.

were swept aside in the name of national security. In 2005 Congress passed the Real ID Act, which granted unprecedented power to the Department of Homeland Security, the federal agency charged with protecting the nation's borders. Thanks to the Real ID Act, nearly fifty different laws were waived by this agency to build portions of structures along the border. It would be the largest waiver of federal laws in the nation's history.

As a direct result of the Real ID Act, by 2016, more than 650 miles (1,046 km) of border has a wall or pedestrian fence, including most of the border between Arizona and Sonora. During the construction, officials conducted no environmental reviews, or assessments to lessen impacts to wildlife or natural or cultural resources. The federal government waived the Endangered Species Act, the Clean Water Act, and the Clean Air Act. Other major laws, such as the American Indian Religious Freedom Act, which protects the heritage of Native Americans, were waived to build the wall. In some instances, land owned by private citizens was seized by the federal government to build portions of the wall. The land was divided, roads were built, and—in many parts along the border—the wall went up. Once again, wildlife and other natural resources were overlooked in the name of national security.

Since 2017 the Trump Administration has enthusiastically emphasized completing the border wall. Much of its effort has been focused on replacing existing vehicle barriers and other permeable fencing, which allow for jaguars and other wildlife to pass freely, with 30-foot-tall (9.1 m) steel and concrete walls. The changes would effectively cut off any movements for wildlife across the US-Mexico border.

By summer 2020, the US constructed more than 200 miles (322 km) of impenetrable walls in areas where vehicle barriers once existed. Many sections of this new wall construction run through areas of sprawling wildlife habitat—areas that the Environmental

Protection Agency once protected. One of these areas is the Organ Pipe Cactus National Monument in southern Arizona, and another is the San Bernardino National Wildlife Refuge along the Arizona–New Mexico border. In Texas, new wall construction cuts through the Lower Rio Grande Valley National Wildlife Refuge. Each of these new sections effectively eliminates safe passage of wildlife across the US-Mexico border.

NEGLECTED

Missing from the heated politics and sensational headlines about the border wall are the native wildlife. These species regularly need to move from place to place, regardless of an international border. Building an impenetrable wall—and the roads, fences, lighting, and traffic that go with the wall—will have devastating effects on local wildlife, from snakes and turtles, to deer and bobcats.

A 2017 study found ninety-seven species of plants and animals that are directly affected by the existing border wall. Several of these species are critically endangered and at risk of going extinct, never to be seen again. Among them are the arroyo toad (*Anaxyrus californicus*), black-spotted newt (*Notophthalmus meridionalis*), and Pacific pond turtle (*Clemmys marmorata*). Also on this infamous list is the jaguarundi (*Herpailurus yagouaroundi*), a small cousin of the jaguar that sometimes wanders north from Mexico and into Texas. A border wall stretching from coast to coast will ensure a jaguarundi never crosses into the United States again.

It's not just threatened and endangered species that will be devastated by a complete border wall. Common bird species like the burrowing owl (*Athene cunicularia*) and cactus ferruginous pygmy owl (*Glaucidium brasilianum cactorum*) are low-flying species. A border wall can severely disrupt the habitats these species rely on. Large, wide-ranging animals such as mule deer (*Odocoileus hemionus*) and bighorn sheep will be prevented from roaming for food and water. Waterways, such as creeks and rivers, will be disrupted as well, affecting the habitats of sensitive desert fish such as the loach minnow (*Tiaroga cobitis*) and Gila chub (*Gila intermedia*).

Even the top predator of the Borderlands—the jaguar—would be no match for the border wall. An impenetrable wall along the US-Mexico border would deny the jaguar its historic range in the United States.

If the border wall were to be built to completion, it would interrupt the habitats of over 1,500 plants and animals, including 62 critically endangered species.

CHAPTER 3

A FRAGMENTED LAND

In 2015 video from a camera trap in the Santa Rita Mountains of the Sky Islands of Arizona captured a male jaguar lazily meandering through oak vegetation. The video quickly went viral. The footage, along with other videos of the same male cat in the Sky Islands, proved that jaguars weren't just occasionally roaming across the Arizona-Mexico border. They were actually *living* in the United States.

The video was featured on newscasts across the nation, and this jaguar became known as El Jefe—Spanish for "the boss." El Jefe has since become a legend in the Borderlands. Video footage of El Jefe has been viewed more than one hundred million times, and a mural in downtown Tucson celebrates the big cat. El Jefe's image adorns T-shirts, and a local beer was even named after the famous jaguar.

To get to the Santa Rita Mountains, El Jefe had to travel from the nearest known breeding population of jaguars, more than 125 miles (201 km) south of the US-Mexico border in the Mexican state of Sonora. The big cat had to hopscotch his way toward the United States, moving from habitat patch to habitat patch across the Sky Islands and adjacent deserts and grasslands. El Jefe made his way into the United States by crossing roads and other physical barriers—and by getting lucky. Very, very lucky. During his trek northward, the big cat had to avoid farmlands where the treeless landscape would expose him. He also had to cross roadways, move around towns and cities, and avoid humans. Despite these challenges, El Jefe is one of the few jaguars that successfully returned to his ancestors' homeland.

But what if El Jefe roamed north hundreds of miles from his birthplace, only to find a giant wall blocking his route to new lands, new mates, and new resources?

ON THE MOVE

Animals and plants need to move to find needed resources and mates. They move because habitats are always changing in space and across time. To escape the cold winter months, when northern lands are covered in snow, birds can migrate hundreds or even thousands of miles southward to be in warmer climates where food and other resources are more easily available. During the dry summer months, deer might move great distances to find more abundant sources of water or forage (the grasses and other plants that range animals feed on). Jaguars and mountain lions might follow these deer, keeping close to their favorite prey. Even plants will slowly change their ranges based on changing conditions such as moisture levels and temperature.

Plants and animals have always had to adapt to the way humans modify and change landscapes. Since the early nineteenth century, the human population on Earth has grown six times in size, ballooning to about 7.3 billion people worldwide. We expand our cities and roadways, and we cut down forests and replace them with farmland to produce more food. We continue to contribute to more and greater habitat loss, subdividing larger pieces of the original landscape into smaller and more isolated patches. This division and habitat loss is known as habitat fragmentation. It can have devastating effects on wildlife and their habitats.

When habitats are fragmented, animals may be unable to move freely across the landscape and acquire needed resources. They may encounter barriers such as towns and cities, roadways and farmland, and fences and walls. Many species cannot, or will not, move across human-altered landscapes. Then plants and animals may be isolated from other members of their species. They may be unable to migrate, seek out needed resources, and find mates as needed during their life cycle.

HABITAT FRAGMENTATION

Many scientists view habitat fragmentation—and the habitat loss that comes with it—as the single greatest threat to preserving the world's biodiversity. Biodiversity is the variety of all life on Earth, from the vast array of birds and mammals to the insect species of all shapes, sizes, and colors throughout the world. It is the different species of trees and plants in the forest. It is everything from the largest elephant to the smallest microbe. Biodiversity also includes genetic diversity, all the genetic material and various traits the species possess. Genetic variation may be the single most important factor that determines whether a population will adapt and persist in a changing environment.

A population is a group of individuals of one species living together in the same area. Each individual in a population has a unique set of genes. These genes are made up of molecules of deoxyribonucleic acid (DNA), the material that provides the instructions for the growth and function of an organism's cells. All organisms, from bacteria to plants and animals, have DNA. DNA is wound up as genes, which express themselves as traits, the characteristics that make each individual vary from one another. Some of these traits are easy to see, such as hair color or height. They can also determine muscle mass, bone density, or quality of eyesight. Other traits are not so obvious, such as a vulnerability to a disease such as diabetes or cancer. Genetic traits are inherited, or passed down from parents to offspring.

MENDEL'S PEAS

The science of heredity explains why you might have your father's hair color and your mother's height. These genes—these traits—were inherited from your parents.

Born in what later became the Czech Republic, Gregor Mendel (1822–1884) was a monk who used the scientific method for simple garden experiments to study heredity. Living in a monastery, Mendel was fond of gardening, and he was baffled by the diversity of plants he grew. Why did some plants of the same species have purple flowers, while others had yellow flowers? Why were some of their seeds round, while others were wrinkled?

With his simple garden experiments, Mendel was about to crack the code of heredity. His test subject was the average garden pea, a vegetable that was easy to work with because it grows fast and produces a lot of offspring. During his experiments, he grew thousands of plants and took meticulous notes. He formulated hypotheses and then tested those hypotheses through repeated experimentation.

Mendel discovered dominant genes and recessive genes. He found that these genes—which instruct the plant to exhibit physical traits such as height or flower color—are passed down from parents to offspring. Each parent contributes genes to their young. Mendel found that dominant genes usually appear in each generation of offspring. Recessive genes are more likely to skip generations, showing up in later generations.

Mendel showed that the combination of dominant and recessive genes as well as genetic mutations help create the genetic diversity that defines life on Earth. But during his lifetime, Mendel's colleagues all but ignored his work, never taking the monk too seriously. It wasn't until decades after his death that scientists embraced the groundbreaking discoveries Mendel found in his garden and called him the father of genetics.

DEEP END OF THE GENE POOL

Every population of plants and animals has a gene pool. This pool is made up of all the genetic material from all individuals in a population. The larger the gene pool, the greater the genetic diversity within that population. The greater the genetic diversity in a population, the greater the chances that population will be able to adapt to changes in the environment.

Why? Because the environment is always changing. Disease can wipe out populations. One year there's a lot of food. The next year there may be very little. Predators move in, and predators move out. Animals must adapt, or die trying.

In a large, genetically diverse population, chances are some individuals possess traits that will allow them to survive. This could be traits that make them more resilient to a disease that might kill other individuals in a population. Maybe it's a trait that gives an animal a different fur color so it can hide from predators just a little bit better. Maybe the trait is better eyesight—a critical characteristic for catching prey or escaping predators. A genetically diverse population increases the probability that at least some individuals will survive and pass on those helpful genes to its offspring. A genetically diverse population is a healthy population and a stable population.

DNA Double Helix

strands

Strands
- Phosphate
- Sugar

Base Pairs
- Adenine
- Thymine
- Cytosine
- Guanine

- Hydrogen bond

Deoxyribonucleic acid (DNA) has a double-helix structure. Two strands of phosphates and sugars wind around each other. Four different amino acids—adenine, cytosine, guanine, and thymine—form the connections between the two strands, creating a molecule that looks much like a twisting ladder. Bunches of DNA form genes.

Humans are changing environments faster than ever. We are building more roads and bigger cities, more walls and fences, cutting down forests, and draining wetlands, leading to more and more habitat fragmentation across Earth. These rapid changes can prevent the free movement of plants and animals. As a result, fragmentation is reducing the exchange of genetic material within species, the hallmarks of diverse and stable populations. Without this healthy genetic diversity, populations of plants and animals may be less likely to adapt and survive in the long term.

CASE STUDY: THE FLORIDA PANTHER

If you're ever exploring the scrubby grasslands and swamps of Florida, keep your eyes and ears out for the Florida panther (*Puma concolor coryi*). This oversized small cat is a subspecies of the eastern puma, also known as the mountain lion or cougar. The eastern puma has mostly been extirpated, or locally extinct, in eastern North America. But this one population still survives in Florida, despite human developments such as shopping malls, roads, and houses.

Because the Florida panther is few in numbers, the population has a relatively small gene pool. The Florida panther is not a genetically diverse population, and the panthers that are left in Florida often inbreed. This type of reproduction occurs when closely related individuals mate and produce offspring. Closely related individuals have very similar genes. When they breed, the gene pool doesn't get deeper, or more diverse. It stays pretty much the same.

Widespread inbreeding can lead to significant health problems, especially for a population teetering on the edge of extinction. If one has an inherited trait such as poor eyesight or breathing problems that may inhibit its chance of survival, for example, this trait would likely be passed on to its offspring. Soon more individuals in a population will have these traits, increasing the chances that both parents and their offspring will have them. In robust and diverse populations, these traits

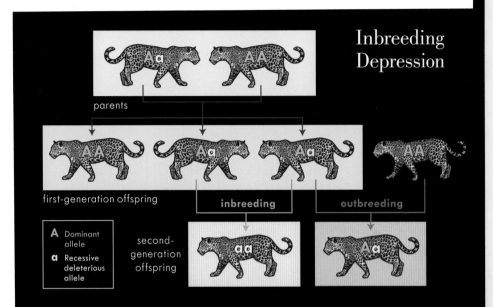

Inbreeding Depression

parents

first-generation offspring

inbreeding

outbreeding

A Dominant allele

a Recessive deleterious allele

second-generation offspring

This diagram shows how inbreeding is more likely than outbreeding to result in offspring that present recessive, deleterious (harmful) traits. Every organism possesses a pair of alleles for every trait: one allele from each parent. Organisms with the alleles AA or Aa will not display the recessive trait, but those with Aa could produce offspring with aa, which will display it. One solution to avoid inbreeding is to introduce more unrelated individuals to the population.

are less likely to be expressed or passed down. But in a small population with a small gene pool, these negative traits are passed from one generation to the next, increasing the likelihood of expression.

Scientists call this reduction in genetic diversity inbreeding depression. In the long term, inbreeding depression can devastate a small population of a species like the Florida panther. If too many individuals eventually inherit and pass on traits that harm the species' ability to survive and adapt, the whole population can become extinct.

Inbreeding depression pushed the Florida panther to the brink of extinction in the early 1990s. By 1994 researchers estimated that fewer than thirty Florida panthers were living there. Wildlife officials found that many of the surviving Florida panthers suffered from heart defects and weak immune systems. These traits were passed from parents to offspring. Some researchers estimated that the Florida panther had a 95 percent chance of becoming extinct if drastic actions were not taken.

Facing the loss of an iconic animal, wildlife biologists implemented a radical, risky idea. In 1995 they translocated—captured and moved—eight female panthers from Texas and released them in southern Florida. Capturing and moving any wild animal, especially a large predator, can be dangerous. Animals easily get stressed when trapped and moved, and lots of things can go wrong along the way. But with well-trained biologists and wildlife managers overseeing the project, the gamble paid off. The panthers from Texas mated and produced offspring with the original population in Florida. The gene pool doubled in size and diversity. The Florida population grew quickly, stabilized by a more diverse gene pool. The negative traits faded away after a few generations. Twenty-five years later, scientists estimate that as many as 230 panthers are surviving in Florida. This is a 700 percent increase in the population in a very short time.

The success of the Florida panther was made possible by the hard work of many dedicated people and organizations. However, with most of the state being surrounded on three sides by water, Florida has limited space to support a large, wide-ranging predator like the panther. Furthermore, the state's human population is among the fastest growing in the nation. As expanding cities and towns continue to fragment the large swaths of habitat the panther needs to survive, the cat is forced into smaller and smaller patches of habitat. Without a nearby population of panthers with which to mate and exchange genes, the population may still be doomed to extinction in the not-too-distant future.

CORRIDORS KEEP IT CONNECTED

The Florida panther's world is a patchwork of landscapes. Patches of panther habitat are separated by modern-day Florida—roads, farms, strip malls, and everything in between. The panther must be able to move safely between these habitat patches. In our ever-changing world, maintaining connectivity between habitat patches is more important than ever. To ensure the safe passage of animals, science is increasingly looking toward wildlife corridors.

Wildlife corridors are habitats that connect wildlife populations. They provide species a way to travel safely between the areas in which they can survive and reproduce, thereby linking patches of habitat that otherwise might have been separated through fragmentation.

Corridors come in all shapes and sizes. A river running through a desert provides a lush corridor for plants and animals. A small patch of forest might allow animals to move through a housing development. A narrow hedgerow bordering a farm may allow animals to avoid open areas when crossing large agricultural fields. A sprawling mountain range offers a green highway for birds to migrate north and south across a continent. Humans even build artificial corridors that cross over bridges and pass through tunnels so animals can move safely over or under highways. We also might restore or protect a patch of forest to protect an important corridor for a large animal such as the jaguar.

Species use corridors for a variety of reasons. They can use them for daily movements from one habitat patch to another to search for food and other resources. They might use corridors for seasonal migrations to move hundreds of miles across continents. But humans can change a landscape so rapidly and so deeply that large areas of wildlife habitat disappear faster than species can adjust their daily, seasonal, or yearly routines. We are also losing corridors that connect these habitats. This loss is creating islands of habitat, where entire populations are isolated from one another, cut off and unable to interbreed.

CHAPTER 4

THE MEN WHO STUDIED ISLANDS

In 1831 twenty-two-year-old Charles Darwin left England for a journey around the world that lasted more than five years. The journey would change how humans view life on Earth and our role within the natural world. As the official naturalist on the sailing ship the HMS *Beagle*, Darwin recorded and collected the animals and plants he encountered during journeys to far-off regions such as the South Pacific, New Zealand, South Africa, and Brazil. He was especially interested in the flora and fauna of the Galápagos Islands, a small collection of islands off the coast of Ecuador in South America. The initial result of these travels was a very successful travelogue, *The Voyage of the Beagle*, published in 1845. Darwin's tales of travels to exotic places to see and record strange plants and animals captivated readers in England. Darwin soon became a star.

During his adventures, and over the next decade at home in England, Darwin thought and wrote about what he had seen, especially the diversity of life he found on the many islands he visited. Like other naturalists of that time, he wanted to understand how species survived and adapted to their environments.

Darwin believed that all life had descended from one common ancestor, rather than appeared through a divine act of creation. He thought and wrote about this natural process, which he called "descent with modification" in which individuals pass traits on to their offspring. Over many generations, those small genetic changes from one generation to the next could eventually cause big changes for a species as a whole. And these changes might mean the difference between survival and extinction. Individuals with traits that are more suited to their environment are more likely to survive, reproduce, and pass on those traits to their offspring. When such patterns occur over generations, all individuals of a species will have these traits, which then become fixed in populations. Ultimately, Darwin wrote, descent through modification can also lead to entirely new species, or evolution.

Darwin believed that the key to understanding how life evolves was found on islands. There, entire communities of plants and animals were isolated from one another. Islands, Darwin thought, are simplified ecosystems, where changes are obvious and observable. Islands were large living laboratories where one could observe these changes in action.

The living laboratory Darwin used to explain his theory of evolution was the Galápagos Islands. There, Darwin studied finches and found that the finches varied from island to island. They were closely related but looked and acted differently depending on what type of habitat they were living in. Some had large beaks to crack open hard nuts. Others had smaller beaks, easier for catching tiny insects. One

1. Geospiza magnirostris.   2. Geospiza fortis.
3. Geospiza parvula.   4. Certhidea olivasea.

This illustration, produced by one of Charles Darwin's contemporaries, shows some of the finches that Darwin observed on the Galápagos Islands. The finches likely all descended from a common ancestor that arrived at the islands thousands of years ago. Different populations of the same species developed different beak shapes and functions, depending on their food source. Over generations, the changes were significant enough that the populations had become different species.

species even learned to use a tool—a cactus spine used to stab grubs and other invertebrates.

Darwin concluded that the fourteen species of finches all evolved from one common ancestor that arrived on the islands many years before. As the original population of finches spread out across the Galápagos Islands, they began to exploit different niches—or parts of their environment. Over time—and many, many generations—small modifications in the finches' gene pool were expressed and advantageous traits were passed down to their offspring. These

DISTRIBUTION

Distribution refers to the geographic range or areas in which a species is found. Many things can influence species distribution, such as the quality of habitat available in a particular area, climate, availability and types of food, or barriers that might prevent movement of the species.

differences between finches that Darwin observed would provide strong evidence to support his theory of evolution.

In 1859, after years of studying the animals of the Galápagos, Darwin published his groundbreaking work, *On the Origin of Species by Means of Natural Selection.* In this large volume, he outlined his theory of evolution and how species change over time through natural selection. This is sometimes called survival of the fittest, where those best adapted to their environment will survive and pass genes on to their offspring. Almost overnight, *On the Origin of Species* changed how we viewed life on Earth.

WHERE THE ANIMALS ARE (AND WHERE THEY ARE NOT)

Through his theory of evolution, Darwin explained *how* species get to be the way they are. Nearly one hundred years later, another theory would help explain how species got to be *where* they are. Biogeography is the study of where animals are—and, conversely, where they are not. Along with the scientific fields of evolution and heredity, biogeography is one of the most important concepts for explaining the patterns of life on Earth.

The concept of biogeography had been around since Darwin's time. Yet it did not become widely popular until the 1960s, thanks to two young Ivy League professors. They were Robert MacArthur, a mathematician and ornithologist (someone who studies birds), and biologist Edward Osborne (E. O.) Wilson, a Harvard graduate who studied ants in the South Pacific. At their core, MacArthur and Wilson were ecologists, or biologists that study how species interact with their environment.

Like Darwin before them, MacArthur and Wilson also studied islands and observed the patterns of life there. The duo's 1967 book, *The Theory of Island Biogeography*, is one of the most important works to explain patterns of species diversity on Earth.

COMMUNITY DYNAMICS

MacArthur and Wilson theorized that island communities eventually reach a balance—an equilibrium—through the two competing forces of immigration (species move into an island) and extinction (other species move out of the island). These two competing forces will maintain the number of species the island can support—the equilibrium.

Species are constantly on the move to find new habitats and new resources. Once organisms discover an island, species begin to immigrate to the island. Birds and insects fly to the island. Small mammals or reptiles might arrive by swimming or even riding a mass of debris set adrift on the water during a storm. Winds may carry seeds and small insects to the island.

There, species will begin to compete for a niche, a role in the ecosystem. For a community of birds, sparrows might become the main seed eaters, and hummingbirds the primary pollinators. Warblers will compete with other birds to gobble up small insects, while shorebirds patrol the beach for small crabs. Birds of prey, such as hawks and owls, will quickly rise to the top of the food chain. Food, water, mates, shelter, and territory are limited on an island. Winners and losers will emerge. On a smaller island—with less area and fewer resources— competition to occupy niches is especially fierce. And with higher levels of competition come higher rates of extinction.

Through their research, MacArthur and Wilson found that islands that are closer to large continents experience high levels of immigration. This makes sense. Large continents host more biodiversity and are a natural source of species that will populate nearby islands. Islands farther away from a large continent will have fewer species because they are more difficult to reach.

MacArthur and Wilson also found that the diversity of species on an island was directly linked to the size of the island. Larger islands have more space and more resources to support a greater number of species. Smaller islands, with less area and fewer resources, support a fewer number of species and therefore have lower biodiversity. Smaller islands also have higher rates of extinction because competition for fewer resources is so intense. Without enough resources to go around, some species will die out.

THE LEGACY OF ISLAND BIOGEOGRAPHY

The scientific community quickly embraced MacArthur and Wilson's simple yet groundbreaking theories soon after their publication. Ecologists soon began applying the concepts spelled out in *Island Biogeography* to other types of isolated ecosystems with limited or unique biodiversity. They referred to these isolated habitats as virtual islands because they aren't actually islands, yet they share similar features, such as being ecologically isolated from other ecosystems. Caves became virtual islands, as did mountaintops. Many ecologists view patches of desert or forest divided by human development as virtual islands too. Even large preserves and national parks are considered islands of biodiversity.

Scientists have also begun to understand that the devastating effects of habitat fragmentation and habitat loss are creating virtual islands. And these islands are everywhere: They are small patches of green in urban landscapes. They are in rural areas divided by roads and agricultural fields. And they are mountain ranges like the Sky Islands, where mountaintop peaks are separated by cities and farmlands, and where jaguars roam. Understanding all these different habitats as virtual islands has helped conservationists in their work to protect biodiversity and save endangered species from extinction.

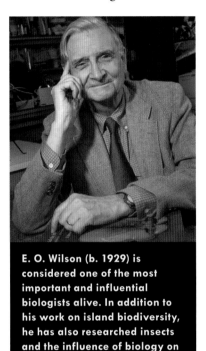

E. O. Wilson (b. 1929) is considered one of the most important and influential biologists alive. In addition to his work on island biodiversity, he has also researched insects and the influence of biology on human culture.

CHAPTER 5

HOW TO PUT THE WORLD BACK TOGETHER

The things that McArthur and Wilson observed decades ago on small tropical islands are occurring throughout the world. As humans fragment more and more of the planetary landscape, we create more virtual islands of habitat separated by roads and cities, farmlands, copper mines, and border walls and, in turn, reduce the important connections between wildlife populations.

In North America, no place is witnessing MacArthur and Wilson's theories play out in real life quite like the Sky Islands region of the Borderlands. There, about twenty-seven different mountain ranges act as islands of mountaintop habitats, stepping-stones of isolated habitat patches, hopscotching from northern Mexico deep into Arizona. In between are vast cities, highways, a border wall, and other barriers preventing the movement of plants and animals.

IT'S ALL CONNECTED

MacArthur and Wilson's theories on island biogeography—and many other contributions that followed—eventually turned the focus to a growing idea in the field of ecology: wildlife corridors. MacArthur and Wilson's ideas highlighted the reality that everything is connected. By using wildlife corridors, individuals and entire populations of species move from habitat to habitat, exchanging genetic material in a constant flow across landscapes.

MacArthur and Wilson's work helped lead to the field of landscape ecology, the study of spatial patterns across ecosystems. The field of landscape ecology examines how different ecosystems interact on a larger scale: the mountains, the rivers, the farmlands, and the cities—they're all connected in a greater landscape. The goal of landscape ecology is to better understand how these landscape features—and how they change—can affect things like wildlife populations or the water cycle.

With the invention of the personal computer in the 1970s, quantitative ecology became widespread. Robust computer programs using the latest in mathematics and statistics allowed ecologists and other scientists to work with huge amounts of data to better identify and understand changes to plant and wildlife populations. Then geographic information systems (GIS) came along in the 1980s. These powerful mapping tools use satellite imagery and radar to gather, store, and analyze geographical data. With advances in GIS and other technologies, ecologists were better able to see the planet as a series of connected landscapes.

GOOD DATA

All good science begins with good data, and the field of ecology is no exception. Data are collected facts, information, or values, such as numbers or measurements. Researchers collect data from various sources, analyze it, and then interpret it to understand what the data means. Data is all around us, every day. Websites collect data on visitors and customers to understand their habits so the websites can provide and advertise things that people want. Police collect data on crime and crime rates to identify problem areas in a community. Transportation authorities collect data on the number of vehicles using a highway to identify where new ones or expansion projects are needed. Instagram, Facebook, Snapchat, and other social media collect data too.

Good data is critical in protecting wildlife and their habitats. In the case of the jaguar, scientists use data to understand the big cat's habits, its habitat needs, and how it moves through the landscape. With this data, conservationists can predict connectivity, or the ability of a species to move between patches of habitat. This information can then be used to identify areas to protect and to find—or create—corridors that jaguars and other wildlife might use.

To measure connectivity, biologists rely on empirical data, or data that researchers collect through observation and measurement. When studying jaguars, empirical data can come from historical records, rigorous field studies, and expert advice. These data can give biologists a better understanding of the jaguar.

Historical records have always been an important source of data for understanding jaguars. These records include all the verified accounts of the big cat collected from old written reports, news stories, and photographs—even from jaguar pelts that hunters brought in decades

CONSERVATION CONNECTION
CONNECTIVITY
Connectivity is a concept biologists use to determine the connections within a landscape. Areas with a lot of barriers, such as fences, roads, or farmlands, have low connectivity. Areas with lots of open spaces have high connectivity.

ago. When researchers compile this information, they learn more about where jaguars have been found in the past, what habitats they prefer, the sex and age of the cats, and so on.

Field data is the information that researchers gather from studies that specifically examine a species in its natural environment. These data can come from a variety of rigorous field studies that track an animal. For example, jaguar scat studies—or examinations of jaguar poop—rely on dogs to find scat left behind by the big cat. Lab technicians study the scat samples to learn about the cat's diet. Genetic sampling of this material can also illuminate answers about a population, such as which individuals are closely related.

Radio collaring is another way to collect important data in the

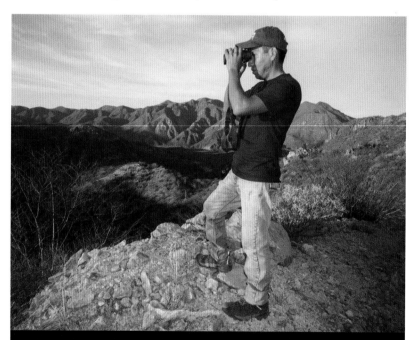

Miguel Gómez, a biologist working at the Northern Jaguar Project (NJP), scans the mountainous landscape of Sonora, Mexico. As a researcher and conservationist, he is responsible for collecting and analyzing various forms of data to help protect jaguar populations.

field. For this method, field-workers capture a jaguar, sedate it, and fit a radio collar around its neck. The collar sends out radio waves that advanced satellite technology picks up and sends to research computers. Researchers can follow the movements of the collared cat without having to actually be in the field. Of course you have to capture the jaguar first, not a simple task. Handling any live animals is often risky to the biologists and especially to the animal.

To avoid these risks, biologists are increasingly turning to remote camera traps to survey for jaguars and other elusive wildlife. These remote cameras, also called trail cameras or game cameras, are set up in hard-to-reach areas—areas where jaguars and other wildlife are known to inhabit. The cameras are often motion-triggered—they snap

Data helps biologists determine where jaguars are more likely to appear, which are also the best places to install camera traps (*inset*). Those camera traps then collect even more data for scientists like Miguel Gómez to analyze.

photos only when something passes in front of a sensor. Camera traps are often set up in movement areas, such as a streambed, or a place where animals are known to visit, such as next to a pond. Using camera traps is a simple and noninvasive way to survey big cats to learn about their habitat preferences and how they move through the landscape. It's also a much less dangerous way to understand a secretive animal. Camera trap studies can provide valuable data, such as how many species live in a certain area or the animal's population density.

Expert advice is key empirical data. Conservationists, biologists, and other people who study jaguars add what they have learned over the years to the larger body of research. Very few people work directly with jaguars, so biologists don't understand everything about this mysterious big cat. However, biologists borrow information from studies on other similar species to make assumptions about jaguars. For example, mountain lions in the American Southwest are plentiful, and many researchers study them. What they know about this large carnivore—such as habitat, prey preferences, and how far the cat will travel—can often be applied to jaguars.

CONSERVATION CONNECTION
POPULATION DENSITY

Population density is the number of individuals of the same species living in a defined area. Scientists use population density to help understand how many individuals of a population can survive in a certain area.

LINKING THE LANDSCAPE

One way researchers use the data is to create predictive models. "Modeling is a prediction of what might happen," says Juan Carlos Bravo, a biologist with the Wildlands Network, a nonprofit group of scientists and policy experts working to protect habitats for Borderlands wildlife such as the jaguar. "Can an animal move in this direction or that direction? What happens when an obstacle is placed here? What happens when a city grows; what happens if the border wall goes up?"

Biologists studying jaguar habitat might start with a map, usually aerial images captured by satellite. These aerial photographs can show the smallest detail in the most remote areas. The photos are then digitized on a computer, where each pixel is assigned a value based on certain characteristics. To model jaguar habitat, the value of each pixel might relate to what researchers already know about the cat's habitat likes and dislikes. These include habitat characteristics such as the types of trees in the forest where the jaguar lives, the amount of canopy cover (leaves at the top of the forest), distance from water, distance from roadways, ruggedness of the terrain, and other factors that might determine where big cats roam.

Predictive models are built with software that uses algorithms, or complex calculations of variables, to sort, search, and otherwise structure large amounts of information. The algorithms assign value to each pixel based on habitat characteristics researchers have prioritized. This sorted information helps researchers identify the habitats the jaguars like best. The model can also show higher-quality habitat versus lower-quality habitat. It can show areas that link one habitat patch to another, identifying corridors that a jaguar is likely to travel from one habitat patch to another.

CONSERVATION CONNECTION
SPECIES RICHNESS
Species richness refers to the number of different species living in a certain area. Biologists track species richness to understand the level of biodiversity in an area.

Ultimately, predictive models help biologists come up with conservation strategies. The models help them decide where to spend money and how to use their resources to protect the jaguar and its habitats. Taking empirical data (what we know about the species) and plugging it into a predictive model (what we *think* we know about the species) can highlight the areas that conservationists should focus on.

"Say the model tells you that there are several mountain ranges that the jaguar would find to be ideal conditions in central or northern Arizona," says Bravo. "What you want to do is first ensure those mountain ranges are protected now and into the future. Then you want to make sure the corridors needed to reach those mountain ranges remain open and protected too."

In 2015 the USFWS and the Wildlife Conservation Society collaborated to identify areas to study in the jaguar's northernmost territory along the Arizona-Mexico border. The team compiled specific data on the jaguar's habitat preferences. The modeling produced valuable maps highlighting which habitats jaguars might use as corridors as they move northward through the Sky Islands and into the United States. This study allowed conservationists to see the landscape as a series of connected landscapes and barriers across which the jaguar moves.

Bravo points out that studying animal behavior on a large scale rather than on a limited basis is important. "When you study the landscape at a regional scale, you get a better understanding of how the planet works as a whole as a collection of systems that maintain life," says Bravo. "You have a prediction of where you want to invest in protecting habitat, in protecting and keeping corridors open."

CASE STUDY: PATH OF THE PRONGHORN

The pronghorn (*Antilocapra americana*) is the fastest land mammal in North America. An adult pronghorn can run up to 55 miles (89 km) per hour. Much like the jaguar, the pronghorn is a relic from a much wilder era, a time when the American West was not restrained by fences, roads, and border walls.

The pronghorn is a migratory animal. Giant herds move hundreds of miles to find water and forage. The animal's range extends from southern Canada through the western plains states of the United States and southward into northern Mexico. Like the jaguar, the pronghorn needs large swaths of connected landscapes to seek out food and mates and to move to where conditions are most suited for survival.

Much like the American buffalo (*Bison bison*), pronghorn populations suffered greatly as European settlers flocked to the American West during the 1800s. While overhunting pushed the buffalo to the brink of extinction, the pronghorn suffered nearly as much. Prior to the arrival of European settlers, up to thirty-five million pronghorn roamed western North America. By 1924, after about a century of European settlement and overhunting in the West, fewer than twenty-four thousand pronghorn remained in the wild.

Unregulated hunting nearly wiped out the pronghorn, but other forces greatly contributed to its population crash too. Settlers brought cattle and other livestock with them. They fenced their ranches to mark property boundaries, to keep their animals from wandering away, and to protect their property from wild predators. By the early 1900s, the American West was crisscrossed with barbed-wire fencing.

For a land-based migratory herd animal such as a pronghorn, fences and other barriers can severely disrupt populations that must roam long distances to find enough resources to survive. Pronghorn are built for speed, not for leaping over obstacles. Because of fences and other forms of habitat loss, pronghorn migration routes were restricted or cut off altogether. This prevented the pronghorn from moving seasonally out of harsh winter conditions on the northern plains. As a result, pronghorn populations declined dramatically.

During the mid-twentieth century, pronghorn populations began to bounce back. Wildlife management and new hunting laws stopped the slaughter of pronghorn. The widespread use of wildlife-friendly fencing—allowing animals to move under barbed-wire fencing—contributed to this recovery as well. Hunting and conservation groups along with state and federal governments also rallied together to preserve large swaths of land as pronghorn migration corridors.

Good science and good data played a critical role in ensuring the pronghorn's future. Advanced modeling techniques helped to identify critical pronghorn corridors. They also identified pinch points, or areas where pronghorn migration slowed or stopped altogether. By 2000 the recovery of pronghorn in the American West was miraculous. Twenty years later, more than one million pronghorn live in the West, mostly in Wyoming and Colorado.

CUT OFF

But parts of the pronghorn range have been forgotten. The Sonoran pronghorn (*Antilocapra americana sonoriensis*) is the southernmost

Due to habitat loss and population decreases, the overall range of the jaguar has diminished considerably over the past century. Conservation efforts help animals like the jaguar regain their former range. The jaguar's huge historic range provides some hope that the jaguar may be able to adapt to living alongside humans as well as it has to vastly different environments.

subspecies of North American pronghorn. It lives in the Borderlands region of Arizona and Mexico. Like the jaguar, the Sonoran pronghorn lives on the very edge of its species range.

Estimates suggest that thousands of years ago, Sonoran pronghorn probably numbered in the millions. In the twenty-first century, only about 1,300 Sonoran pronghorn still live in the Borderlands region. With more roads and fences and a possible extension of the border wall, the Sonoran pronghorn population will become even more cut off. The herds will be unable to move freely north and south across the border.

The portion of the US-Mexico border that runs through Sonoran pronghorn territory is mostly marked with a vehicle barrier. Unlike a wall or fence, this type of barrier involves rails and piping, fortified to prevent vehicles from passing through. Vehicle barriers still allow for pronghorn and some other larger wildlife animals to pass through.

Other more elusive animals such as jaguars will avoid the traffic altogether. And replacing vehicle barriers with large and more impenetrable fencing or walls would permanently divide the Sonoran populations. This could lead to greater isolation, greatly reducing genetic diversity and the probability of the animal's long-term survival, and thus dooming the Sonoran pronghorn to extinction.

CHAPTER 6

SAFE HAVEN, SAFE PASSAGE

The foothills of the Sierra Madre in Sonora, Mexico, are a several-hour drive south of the US-Mexico border. In this wild and remote area lives the northernmost population of Borderlands jaguars. Big cats in this region sometimes wander north and are occasionally spotted in the United States. Here too is the Northern Jaguar Reserve, a sprawling protected area of land set aside for the jaguar and many other wildlife. The reserve and the surrounding lands provide more than 55,000 acres (223 sq. km) of rugged, mountainous habitat, free from many of the threats to jaguars' survival, such as hunting, trapping, and busy roads or development. The protected area of the reserve is in the heart of the northernmost breeding population of jaguars at the very edge of the species' range. These cats occasionally roam north across the US-Mexico border.

The Northern Jaguar Reserve protects some of the jaguar's range. Jaguars are free to move in and out of the reserve.

Since 2003 the Northern Jaguar Project, a Tucson-based nonprofit organization, has been working to protect this critical habitat for this population of big cats. Miguel Gómez is the reserve's manager. Along with his wife, Carmina Gutiérrez, he manages a massive network of about 150 remote camera traps scattered throughout the reserve and the surrounding ranches. Each month Miguel and Carmina visit the cameras with the help of cowboys, or vaqueros. The team usually travels by 4x4 truck, driving along old ranching roads that haven't been maintained for years. The roads—if you can call them roads—are riddled with jagged rocks and boulders. A flat tire is a regular occurrence here. And if you get a flat, no one is coming to help. You're on your own. Although these roads might prevent humans from visiting, it's the perfect, wild landscape for the jaguar to roam.

Miguel and Carmina will spend more than a week driving to and then hiking steep hillsides and rocky canyons to check on the cameras and retrieve photographs. They set up camp, and each night, the two get out a laptop computer to review the images.

The photographs from the camera traps reveal a fascinating look at the wild lives of animals. In any given month, the hidden cameras capture creatures in their natural environments: a pair of ocelots sharpening their claws on a downed tree, a family of mountain lions taking an afternoon nap, a troop of coatimundis (members of the raccoon family) traipsing down the wash. There are black-tailed deer and peccaries, roadrunners, bobcats, and skunks. The results showcase the reserve's wildness and biological diversity.

One day, a camera produced a new image of Chiltepin, an adult male jaguar named after a local pepper plant common to this part of Mexico. Chiltepin has been photographed several times in recent months, passing through a dry riverbed not far from the team's camp. Humans, whether a casual hiker or the most fearless biologist, rarely see actual jaguars in the wild. As big and powerful as they are, jaguars move like ghosts through the reserve's thick thornscrub habitat. That's why camera traps are such a valuable tool to understanding these elusive cats.

Chiltepin as photographed by a camera trap in the Northern Jaguar Reserve

"We use the remote cameras for monitoring the jaguars and ocelot movements in the area," Miguel explains. The images of jaguars and ocelots captured by the camera traps tell researchers about the different species of cats on the reserve. "[Individual] cats are recognizable because of their spot pattern. We also use the data of other feline species—puma and bobcat." The data collected by these photos can tell the biologists how many cats live on the reserve and how these species use the available habitats.

WORKING TOGETHER

NJP has been very successful in protecting this large swath of land for the northern population of jaguars. But it wasn't always like this. These

successes took years of hard work by many dedicated individuals. Part of the NJP's conservation strategy involves the local community in protecting jaguars and other cats. But this took changing minds and earning trust. Ranching is part of the very fabric of the communities in northern Mexico. For generations, ranchers viewed the jaguar as the enemy, a giant predator that wouldn't hesitate to kill a calf or cow or even a person. Ranchers or their hired hunters, known as *cazadores* in Spanish, regularly shot and killed jaguars and mountain lions. This is still common in the Borderlands of northern

Carmina Gutiérrez, NPJ's research coordinator, examines a camera trap at the NJP.

Mexico. In the last decade many jaguars have been killed in the region, including females with cubs. Yet some local ranchers still think of it as necessary for protecting property, livestock, and a traditional way of life.

Changing minds and forging relations with the local community took years. Initially, NJP purchased a ranch with more than 10,000 acres (40.5 sq. km) of pristine habitat. This would become the heart of the reserve. The project began by removing the cattle from the lands and banning hunting. Cattle had overgrazed the lands, degrading the areas and leaving it stripped of grasses and other vegetation. Overhunting, meanwhile, removed many of the jaguar's prey base, such as deer and peccaries. With the cattle removed, vegetation soon came back and thrived. With no hunting, prey species soon bounced back as well.

Although this initial parcel of land seemed like a lot of space, a healthy population of jaguars needs more room to thrive. *A lot* more room. NJP needed to expand the reserve to protect the surrounding areas that would provide enough space for the big cat to thrive. "The Reserve is not big enough to protect a jaguar population," Miguel explains. "We have to work with the local ranches to protect safe areas and safe corridors for the northernmost jaguar population."

In 2007 NJP established a program called Viviendo con Felinos (Living with Cats). It works to forge trusting relations with the community of ranchers, some of whom have been working these lands for generations. NJP convinced ranchers that jaguars and other predators were not the enemy. They were part of the natural landscape, part of the heritage of Sonora. One by one, local ranchers bought into the Viviendo program.

In regions where livestock ranching is at odds with wildlife, local governments will sometimes pay ranchers if predators such as jaguars and mountain lions kill their cattle or other livestock. NJP turned this idea upside down with a new model of conservation. In the program,

A rancher participates at a community celebration of the NJP's Viviendo program in Sahuaripa, Sonora, Mexico.

NJP pays ranchers for photos of cats. When a rancher agrees to become part of Viviendo, NJP biologists like Miguel and Carmina set up a series of camera traps around the ranch. In return, the rancher agrees to ban hunting on their property, letting both cats and prey species return to the land.

Every month or so, Miguel and Carmina travel to each ranch, retrieving the images from the remote cameras and paying the ranchers. A photo of a bobcat earns the rancher 500 pesos (about $28). A photo of a mountain lion earns 1,000 pesos (about $55), while ocelots earn 1,500 pesos (about $83) per photo. Each photo of a jaguar earns the rancher 5,000 pesos (about $276). With the Viviendo program, taking photos of cats is more profitable than compensation for livestock lost through predation by a jaguar or mountain lion.

Seventeen ranchers participate in the program, and more are joining. Since 2007 more than fifty different jaguars have been photographed on these lands and the ranches in the Viviendo program.

"It has been a long way to change the perspective of some ranchers toward felines, specifically the jaguar," says Miguel. "Now we can say we have made a positive change with our neighbors, and now they are allies in this conservation project."

SOURCES

The Northern Jaguar Reserve is a refuge, a protected place where the northernmost big cat population can remain stable, free from the threats of urban sprawl and hunting. The reserve is also a critical link to other populations of jaguars that live about 200 miles (322 km) farther south in Mexico. These lands are part of the genetic highway that links all the jaguar populations between North and South America.

Only about 4.3 percent of Earth's land is protected in places such as the Northern Jaguar Reserve, national parks, and wildlife refuges. These protected areas can help stabilize source populations of species at risk, but they are not the only solution—and they are not enough. In any population, including humans, the reproduction rate can outpace the death rate. This creates a surplus of individuals in that population. Eventually too many individuals will be competing for limited resources such as food, mates, and territory. Some individuals will need to disperse to areas where more resources are available. These individuals will move to other patches of habitat not occupied by others of their species, where there are more resources and less competition.

If individuals from a source population can't disperse to an area with suitable habitat to ease the competition for resources, the source population—although healthy and stable—will never grow, or expand. The source population will become, in essence, a really big zoo. This is why animals, especially large animals, need to be able to move around, and why habitat fragmentation is such a threat.

CARRYING CAPACITY

Carrying capacity is the maximum population size that a patch of habitat can support. The capacity differs according to the amount of water, food, mates, and resources that are available in that area. An area with more resources can support larger populations, and an area with fewer resources will contain smaller populations. When an area reaches its carrying capacity—when the habitat patch cannot provide enough resources for more individuals—those individuals must go somewhere else to find the resources they need to survive.

CASE STUDY: GRIZZLIES ON THE MOVE

The brown bear (*Ursus arctos*) is the second-largest land animal in North America. Only the polar bear (*Ursus maritimus*) is larger. The brown bear range extends from Alaska through much of western Canada and southward into the United States. North America is home to several subspecies of brown bears. The grizzly bear (*Ursus arctos horriblus*), the most famous of them, is found in northern Rocky Mountain states such as Montana, Idaho, and Wyoming.

Unlike jaguars, which can wander hundreds of miles in search of territory, grizzly bears don't disperse very far from their natal ranges. A male grizzly will disperse an average of about 18 miles (29 km). Females move only about 6 miles (9.6 km) from home. That's not very far for such a large animal. Because they have short dispersal habits, grizzly territories are close to one another so that individuals will meet, mate, and exchange genetic material to maintain healthy populations.

Much of the grizzly bear's North American range is connected by loose populations, like stepping-stones going north and south across the western portion of the continent. One of the North American grizzly populations is in the North Continental Divide Ecosystem (NCDE), a vast area that covers much of Montana and southern Alberta, Canada.

The NCDE population of grizzlies is connected to grizzly populations in far northwestern Canada and westward into Alaska. Corridors and other connected habitats allow the NCDE grizzly population to interact and exchange genes on this genetic superhighway from Montana to Alaska.

However, one population of grizzlies has been separated from the others in the NCDE. The Greater Yellowstone Ecosystem (GYE) of northwestern Wyoming, southwestern Montana, and eastern Idaho covers more than 22,000 square miles (56,980 sq. km) of mountains and sprawling valleys. At the heart of the GYE is Yellowstone National Park, a vast protected area free from hunters and highways. The park is home to a source population of grizzlies. The GYE population is also an isolated population, cut off from other grizzly populations to the north. So the GYE is essentially a genetic island in the middle of the Rocky Mountains.

The grizzly bear was first listed as an endangered species in 1975, when the GYE supported only about 136 bears. Forty-five years later, the grizzly outlook has improved, and the Yellowstone bear was re-listed as threatened. Experts believe the Yellowstone population is somewhere between seven hundred and one thousand grizzlies. However, the landscape around Yellowstone National Park has reached carrying capacity and cannot support more grizzlies. To survive, bears are dispersing northward, farther and farther beyond the protected boundaries of the park.

Just as the GYE population is expanding its range north, the NCDE population is ranging southward for many of the same reasons. By 2017 only about 68 miles (110 km) separated the two populations. While this is great news for grizzly populations, it means that bears are pressing farther into human-dominated landscapes and increasing the risk of conflict—conflicts the grizzly bear rarely wins. Some bears are deemed "problems" because they kill livestock or get into human-populated areas in search of food. Over the decade from 2000 to 2009, sixty-eight problem grizzlies were euthanized by authorities in and around Yellowstone National Park. In recent years the number of grizzlies killed has increased significantly. In 2018 alone, thirty-eight grizzly bears were euthanized. Without areas of safe passage, a growing grizzly bear population increases the risk of conflict between humans and bears.

To help the bears—and reduce conflicts with humans—government agencies, nongovernmental organizations (NGOs), and private landowners are rallying together to ensure safe passage for the grizzly. For example, the Interagency Grizzly Bear Study Team (IGBST) is a group of scientists from various agencies and Native American tribes in grizzly country who study the GYE grizzlies. Between 2000 and 2015, the group radio-collared 124 GYE bears to find out how they disperse. The group used the tracking data to model a series of possible routes the GYE bears might take to connect with the NCDE population.

The data collected by IGBST are providing valuable information. Wildlife experts working with state transportation agencies, which manage the area's highways, have already used the data to identify pinch points where bears are likely to cross roadways outside the park. These efforts can also help create new corridors. Sometimes these corridors can be artificial connections in the landscape like bridges and tunnels that allow wildlife to pass safely over or under roadways. These wildlife crossings allow grizzlies and other animals to move safely across the landscape from one habitat patch to another.

BUILDING BRIDGES

About 800 miles (1,287 km) north of Yellowstone, in Alberta, Canada, sits Banff National Park. Each year Banff draws more than 4 million visitors to its 2,564 square miles (6,641 sq. km) of pristine Canadian Rocky Mountain wilderness. Here you'll find stunning snow-capped mountains and turquoise glacial lakes, dense lodgepole pine forests and lots of wildlife. The expansive Banff wilderness is home to not only the grizzly bear, but also the lynx, wolverine, elk, moose, gray wolf, and black bear—all large species that move around a lot.

Even a massive national park like Banff is not immune to habitat fragmentation. Bisecting the park is the Trans-Canada Highway, a huge four lane roadway that connects Canada coast to coast. More than 50 miles (82 km) of the highway run right through Banff. Although the highway was initially a modest, two-lane road, in 1978 the Trans-Canada Highway expanded to four lanes through the park. While these changes improved traffic for humans, it came at great expense to the park's wildlife. Scientists watched as corridors and migration routes were cut off, core habitats were fragmented into smaller patches, genetic exchange within species fell, and wildlife-vehicle collisions skyrocketed. Something needed to be done. But what? Could the park reconnect these lost linkages?

Banff soon began a grand experiment in reconnecting habitats. During the 1980s, the park created a series of underpasses for wildlife—culverts and tunnels—that allowed for safe passage beneath the busy highway. Then in 1996, the park completed two large wildlife overpasses, bridges that cross over the highway. From the roadway, the overpasses look like ordinary bridges, complete with concrete walls and metal fencing. But these crossings are for wildlife only. No humans allowed. Look closely and you'll see a bridge covered in mature pine trees and thick shrubs, mimicking the natural landscapes found on both sides of the roadway. These overpasses work like natural wildlife corridors, encouraging safe passage across a dangerous highway. The Banff Wildlife Crossings Project has constructed six overpasses and thirty-eight underpasses, resulting is a massive network of artificial wildlife crossings across the park.

To see if animals were actually using the crossings, Banff National Park implemented a long-term monitoring effort. Over seventeen years, scientists used camera traps to monitor each of the forty-four crossing

WILDLIFE-VEHICLE COLLISIONS

Researchers are seeing growing evidence that artificial wildlife crossings have direct benefits—lifesaving benefits—to humans. Wildlife crossings not only allow for safe passage of wildlife, but they can also greatly reduce the risk of wildlife-vehicle collisions (WVCs). Each year WVCs cause about two hundred human deaths and twenty-six thousand major injuries around the United States. The most common WVC is with deer, a large and wide-ranging mammal found throughout North America. Deer WVCs cause up to $8.3 billion in damages each year, mostly to vehicles and in hospital bills from human injuries.

Colorado is home to large deer populations as well as miles of winding mountainous roadways. That can be a dangerous combination for motorists and wildlife alike. In one particular hotspot for WVCs, Colorado Parks and Wildlife teamed up with the state's department of transportation to reduce accidents along Highway 9 northwest of Denver. This 11-mile (17.7 km) stretch of road was notorious for its annual WVCs with deer. In just one twenty-year period, two hundred people were injured and sixteen people died due to WVCs along this small stretch of road. The agencies first worked together to identify "hotspots" along the highway where wildlife like to cross. They then constructed two wildlife overpasses and five underpasses along Highway 9. Finally they installed 8-foot-high (2.4 m) wildlife fencing along each side of the roadway, fencing that prevented wildlife from wandering onto the highway while also guiding the animals towards the safe crossing areas. A five-year monitoring effort showed 83,000 mule deer crossings over the seven installed structures. During the same time period, WVCs dropped more than 90 percent along this dangerous section of highway.

structures. By 2016, researchers had documented more than 200,000 individual animal crossings, mostly large ungulates (hooved animals) such as moose, deer, and elk. That's a lot of large animals that were no longer wandering onto a busy highway. During that same time period, wildlife-vehicle collisions dropped by over 80 percent along the highway.

To find out if the crossings allowed for genetic exchange between populations divided by the highway, scientists collected and genetically analyzed hair samples from wildlife. One study completed by the Western Transportation Institute at Montana State University collected more than ten thousand hair samples, mostly from black bears and grizzly bears. They compared the hair samples collected at the wildlife crossings to other samples from bear populations around the park. Results clearly indicated that the wildlife crossings were helping to maintain the exchange of genetic material across the highway while also reducing genetic isolation among bear populations.

Banff has since become a world-renown success story for wildlife crossings. The park regularly attracts scientists from around the world who come to study the network of overpasses and underpasses. Lessons learned from the Banff Wildlife Crossings Project has helped improve habitat connectivity for gazelle in Argentina, tapirs in Belize, and tigers in China, among many others.

CHAPTER 7

CROSSING BORDERS

The jaguar's range in the Americas spans two continents and eighteen nations. This big cat's realm is distributed across more than 2.3 million square miles (6 million sq. km) of various environments, from arid uplands in the Sky Islands to lowland swamps in Brazil's Pantanal region. Few other predators can claim such wide and diverse landscapes as part of their range.

Throughout the jaguar's range, habitat fragmentation and habitat loss are major threats, forcing the big cat into smaller and smaller areas. Poaching and hunting chip away at large populations in South America and imperil smaller, fragile populations in Sonora. The jaguar has been extirpated from more than 40 percent of its historic range across the Americas. If the big cats are to persist, they need international help. Cooperation and collaboration among nations is key in saving wildlife across continents.

One organization leading the charge across boundaries is Panthera, an international NGO aimed at protecting big cats around the world. Founded by Thomas S. Kaplan and his wife, Daphne Recanati, in 2006, Panthera works in forty-seven nations to protect all species of cats, including snow leopards (*Panthera uncia*) in Asia, cheetahs (*Acinonyx jubatus*) and lions in Africa, and tigers in the Russian Far East. At the center of Panthera's mission is protecting jaguars in the Americas.

A CHAMPION FOR BIG CATS

No person is more associated with jaguar protection than Alan Rabinowitz. Born in Brooklyn, New York, he was a quiet child with a severe stutter. Rabinowitz seemed like the least likely person to become a towering figure in wildlife conservation. His story proves that each person can make a difference.

In college, Rabinowitz studied black bears in the Smoky Mountains of Tennessee. Soon after, a former professor offered him an opportunity to study jaguars in the jungles of Belize. Very few people had ever studied jaguars, and Rabinowitz didn't even know where Belize was. But he jumped at the chance.

Rabinowitz studied jaguars for three years in the dense jungles of Belize. He learned from the local Maya people how to capture jaguars and how to fit them with radio collars. Those years in the jungle weren't easy. He survived a near-fatal plane crash. A field assistant died from a venomous snakebite. His body was weak and riddled with parasites. But he knew he had one thing to do before leaving the country.

Rabinowitz managed to get a private meeting with the leaders of Belize's government. This was Rabinowitz's chance to convince the leaders to protect the jaguar and other wildlife of Belize. Rabinowitz left the meeting with an agreement that

(RE)CONNECTING THE DOTS

Too often, large conservation projects stop at international borders, where governments, laws, cultures, and social priorities might differ between nations. Panthera's Jaguar Corridor Initiative, created by conservationist Alan Rabinowitz, is a large and ambitious project to maintain the connections among ninety separate populations of jaguars that span eighteen nations, from northern Mexico to central Argentina in South America. The initiative brings a continent-wide approach

Belize would create the Cockscomb Basin Wildlife Sanctuary—the world's first jaguar preserve. Around two hundred jaguars live there, one of the largest populations of jaguars in the world. Just through determination, Rabinowitz helped create a massive sanctuary for countless wildlife in the Belize jungle.

Rabinowitz eventually became the chief scientist for Panthera. It aims to protect big cats around the world, but the jaguar was always a personal focus for the world-renown conservationist. Rabinowitz died in 2018 at the age of sixty-four after a long struggle with leukemia. He leaves behind a massive legacy of protecting cats around the world. Rabinowitz's inspirational story also shows that no matter what the obstacles, one person can make a difference.

Rabinowitz (*left*) poses with Howard Quigley, who took over as Panthera's leading scientist after Rabinowitz's death.

to protecting jaguar habitats in an effort to coordinate efforts across borders and get nations to work together to protect the cat. The goal of the initiative is to build partnerships, from local ranching communities to large national governments, to protect jaguar habitats across the cat's entire intercontinental range.

Large swaths of habitat for source populations of jaguars still remain in parts of Mexico and Central and South America. Many are in protected areas, and the initiative's goal is to build and protect wildlife corridors that weave among the ranches, farms, and other private lands in the human-dominated landscape. Then the cats can move from larger source populations into other areas of suitable habitat, allowing the jaguar populations to grow. This requires finding solutions that allow jaguars and humans to coexist, regardless of international borders.

The initiative started when Panthera biologists collaborated with experts across the Americas. They used GIS and remote sensing to model likely pathways that the cat would use for dispersal. The next step was ground-truthing, or verifying that the corridors exist and

Adapted from the organization Panthera's own data, this map shows the enormous network of wildlife corridors that jaguars can use to move between populations. The corridors illustrated in red are at risk of being destroyed. Panthera targets its conservation efforts at these corridors to ensure that no population of jaguars become isolated.

documenting that the prey animals live there. Panthera biologists went to Belize in Central America and to Bolivia and Brazil in South America to examine the corridors firsthand. They set up camera traps to observe the jaguar in its habitat. They also wanted to see if the cats were actually using the corridors the models had identified.

By identifying these critical jaguar habitats, Panthera is implementing different projects on the ground to help protect these areas. These efforts are varied and are based on reducing the most immediate threats to the jaguar: In Guatemala, Panthera is trying to save vanishing jaguar habitat that is being destroyed by poorly managed agricultural practices, such as big farming operations. In Colombia, Panthera is working to designate a new national park in the Serranía de San Lucas, a forested mountain area that is a critical corridor link for jaguars in Colombia. In Brazil, Panthera is focusing on reducing conflicts with ranchers, who can sometimes lose livestock to jaguars and other large predators, a relationship that foments anger toward the big cat.

Friedeberg checks a camera trap.

A main focus of the Jaguar Corridor Initiative is to prioritize protecting the corridor "backbones" that run throughout the Americas. These priority corridors are critical to maintaining connections between populations and the most important habitats that can preserve connectivity throughout the cat's entire range.

"If we lost any parts of this backbone then we are really in trouble," says Diana Friedeberg, director of Panthera-Mexico.

"There are some areas that once lost it is going to be really hard to put back together. If it comes down to, okay, you only have so much time, so much money, where are you going to put these efforts? Then you would put it in the backbone. This is the area with the most hope, the most potential."

In countries like Brazil and Colombia, large portions of jaguar habitat remain wild—even though jaguar habitat is being lost rapidly. For example, in some smaller nations of Central America, vast areas of jaguar habitat have already been lost to deforestation, where farmers and developers cut down wild forest to make room for human activity.

These backbone corridors are most important in Central America, such as in Guatemala and Honduras. The Central American isthmus (a landform with a body of water on two sides) has been a natural wildlife corridor between the North and South American continents for three million years. Yet in recent decades, large farms, plantations, and growing cities and towns fragmented these landscapes and destroyed huge portions of wildlife habitat. And high rates of drug trafficking and other dangerous crimes in the region make it difficult for researchers to study jaguars and protect their habitats. So the jaguar is completely extirpated in some Central American nations like El Salvador. If more Central American nations lose their jaguars, big cats in Mexico to the north will be permanently isolated from those in South America. Once this connection disappears, it will be extremely difficult, if not impossible, to restore it.

TRANSBOUNDARY CONSERVATION

Of course, wildlife like jaguars, pronghorn, or grizzly bears know no boundaries between nations. Known as transboundary conservation, protecting wildlife habitat across international boundaries can be very complicated. It's a delicate balance of politics, policy, culture, and heritage. International neighbors may have very different views about how to protect wildlife and their habitats.

Transboundary conservation in the Borderlands of the United States and Mexico can be exceedingly difficult. Sometimes these differences are embedded in the value each nation puts on wildlife conservation. For example, the United States has a vast, well-funded public lands system. National parks, wildlife refuges, state parks, and other lands provide a sprawling network of territory protected by local, state, and national laws. In addition, taxes from hunting and fishing and other outdoor sporting licenses help pay for conservation and protection. Strict laws such as the Endangered Species Act protect wildlife and their habitats. And the United States has a wide network of nonprofit and community organizations dedicated to conservation. The result is a coast-to-coast effort to protect natural areas while still allowing the public to enjoy them.

Meanwhile, in Mexico, the central government does not manage a large system of public lands. Most land in Mexico is owned by individuals or communities. Known as ejidos, these communal lands are often used for agriculture and are handed down through generations. About 80 percent of the forests and jungles of Mexico are ejidos. Hunting, farming, and mining occur there, even if they are home to vulnerable wildlife species. However, this model of land ownership allows local communities to manage their lands as they see fit. In the United States, faraway government agencies make many of those decisions for citizens.

"Conservation has to be done from the bottom up and from the top down," says Friedeberg. "You have to have local communities to buy in, to believe [in] what they're doing. We have to talk to the people to convince them that conservation is profitable for them, for their future, for their children. Here in Mexico, we work with the communities that actually live in the corridors. That's how we're protecting the corridors."

A game ranger shows off old traps used in jaguar studies at the Cockscomb Basin Wildlife Sanctuary in Belize.

Panthera works with many local leaders, from park officials and teachers to politicians, Indigenous groups, and other conservation programs. Panthera also works with local ranchers and farmers to create model ranches. These working ranches are wildlife-friendly. They may install electric fencing rather than physical barriers to protect livestock from predators. Or they may enforce strict no-hunting rules on certain species on their land. This ensures that jaguars and mountain lions have enough prey animals to hunt so they will not turn to hunting livestock.

ECONOMICS OF CONSERVATION

Conservation programs cost money, sometimes *lots* of money. You have to pay biologists for research and data collection. You have to pay ranchers and cowboys to care for lands for wildlife. You have to buy and take care of camera traps, trucks, fencing, and other equipment.

UMBRELLA SPECIES CONCEPT

The umbrella species concept is a conservation strategy. Experts know that by conserving one particular species, such as the jaguar, a whole host of other species will also benefit. With this concept as a guide, conservations funnel time, money, and effort toward one particular species and its habitats, knowing the impact will be broad, like an umbrella, protecting many other species and habitats.

Money can be even more important in poorer areas of the world. For example, rural areas usually have the highest levels of biodiversity. They are in lands that jaguars roam. And they are often home to the rarest, most threatened plants and animals. Rural areas often struggle economically. Opportunities for education and well-paying jobs can be limited. So the goals of wildlife conservation are sometimes in direct conflict with the economy of a local community. These communities may be under pressure from companies that want to profit off the land—the land jaguars and other wildlife need to survive. For example, a mining company may want to explore for valuable gold or uranium in a pristine mountain wilderness. Perhaps a new hotel is opening in a protected area, an expanding roadway threatens to divide a forest, or a large plantation will cut down thousands of acres of rain forest to replace with palm oil trees.

For farmers or ranchers struggling financially, these offers are tempting. When forced to decide between protecting land that may be home to a couple of jaguars or selling a few acres to provide for their family, protecting the jaguar will often lose.

"In the real world you can't stop development," Friedeberg explains. "You can't stop people from building roads and building hotels. So you try to work with development, to work with these companies." Whatever nation they are working in, Panthera tries to be part of discussions with growing and developing communities. "We are trying to talk to these companies and get into the game with them to make decisions with them. You have to work with everyone, the community, the businesses, everyone."

PALM OIL

One growing threat to the jaguar is the spread of palm oil plantations. Palm oil is the most traded vegetable oil in the world. It is used in a variety of everyday products, from lipstick and laundry detergent to pet food, frozen pizza dough, and sugary snacks like cookies and candy bars. But growing the trees to produce this oil takes a lot of land.

To meet the demand for palm oil, companies are clearing more and more acres of forest and jungle to create palm tree plantations. The plantations are monocultures, agricultural lands that produce only one type of moneymaking crop. Palm oil plantations may be large, green spaces, but they are wastelands for wildlife and biodiversity.

No place is more ravaged by palm oil production than Southeast Asia, where about 85 percent of the world's palm oil is produced. Between 2001 and 2013, production of palm oil doubled, mostly in countries such as Indonesia and Malaysia on the Southeast Asian island of Borneo. In these places, about 667,000 acres (2,699 sq. km) of forest are cleared each year for palm oil production. Since the 1970s, palm oil production has led to 47 percent of deforestation in Indonesia alone. That is a stunning rate of habitat loss in some of the world's most biodiverse landscapes.

One species most threatened by the expansion of palm oil production is the Borneo orangutan (*Pongo pygmaeus*). Like the jaguar, the orangutan is a large species that needs lots of room to roam. It also relies on large blocks of pristine forests—land that is valuable to the lucrative palm oil industry. The unfortunate result of the expansion of palm oil plantations on the island of Borneo is that the orangutan's population is sharply declining—and not strictly due to deforestation. One study found that palm oil workers killed almost 150,000 orangutans since 1999 across the region. The animals' crime? Having lost their forest habitat, the orangutans were starving. They had wandered onto palm plantations in search of food. These conflicts are devastating to orangutan populations. Some studies estimate that Borneo orangutan populations have dropped more than 80 percent since the early 1970s.

CONSUMERS SAY NO

Organizations like the World Wildlife Fund and the Rainforest Action Network have launched successful public awareness campaigns to let the public know what is happening to the orangutan in Southeast Asia. As a result, some big companies are making changes. They are using palm oil cultivated through more sustainable practices, such as only purchasing from palm oil producers that strictly follow local environmental laws and which manage and monitor the production of palm oil. These companies label their products so that consumers know the palm oil comes from sustainable, more eco-friendly sources.

These efforts can be effective because they focus on the economics of the problem. And it's a very simple equation: when consumers refuse to purchase products that use ingredients that harm the environment and wildlife, profits from those products drop. Companies notice. They are more likely to stop using palm oil or switch to more sustainable ingredients. In this global age, the purchases we make in our neighborhood can have rippling effects across the world—even into the exotic jungles of Borneo.

Some studies have shown that these public awareness campaigns can help slow the rate of deforestation in Southeast Asia. A report in 2019 found that expansion of palm oil plantations in Borneo is decreasing, expanding at a rate of 28 percent in 2017 and then 22 percent in 2018. And big business is noticing. Thanks to a grassroots effort started by two teenage sisters, in 2020 cereal producer Kellogg pledged to make its palm oil practices more sustainable. PepsiCo and Nestlé—producers of many popular snacks—also pledged stricter rules on using palm oil.

While these are improvements, there's still a long way to go. As the expansion of the palm oil industry slows in Southeast Asia, some palm oil operations are moving to another part of the world—the Americas. In recent years, countries such as Mexico, Venezuela, and Guatemala have nearly doubled their production of palm oil. Brazil, Costa Rica, and Honduras have increased production by more than 75 percent. Conservationists say this disturbing trend threatens the future of the jaguar and countless other unique wildlife species in the Americas.

CASE STUDY: THE MONARCH HIGHWAY

Protecting wildlife habitats and corridors isn't important only for jaguars and other large, terrestrial (land-based) mammals. Corridors of green space that connect Mexico to the United States and extend into Canada support, for instance, the life cycle of the monarch butterfly (*Danaus plexippus*). Each year, monarch butterflies spend summers in the United States and southern Canada. In the fall, monarchs head south, fluttering in the wind for thousands of miles before reaching their wintering grounds in southern Mexico. There, high in the *oyamel* forests, monarch butterflies gather to spend the winter, creating one of the most spectacular phenomena in the entire animal kingdom, where towering fir trees are literally covered in millions of wintering monarchs.

Like all members of Lepidoptera—the order of insects that includes moths and butterflies—monarch butterflies are pollinators. As adults, they flutter from flower to flower feeding on the sugary nectar produced by the plants. In return, the monarchs pollinate—transfer pollen—from one flower to another, allowing the plant to reproduce. The relationship between plants and pollinators, such as butterflies, benefits both organisms. It is one of the most important relationships in our world because pollinators aid in the reproduction of not just pretty flowers in a garden but a wide variety of food crops such as strawberries, apples, and almonds. Pollinators are directly responsible for 35 percent of all food crops produced around the world. Monarchs, bees, and other small pollinators help support the supply of food we humans depend on.

But monarchs are facing threats from all sides. Illegal logging in Mexico's *oyamel* forests, a key and delicate wintering ground, threatens the survival of the monarch. Data show the impact of this habitat loss. During the 1990s, experts estimated Mexico's wintering population of monarchs to be about one billion. Twenty-five years later, in the winter of 2013–2014, researchers saw that only about thirty-three million monarchs made it to the wintering grounds in Mexico. In 2020 a survey of wintering monarchs in Mexico showed a 53 percent drop in numbers from just the previous year. These are staggering population declines. The situation is so dire that some scientists predicted we could soon lose all monarch butterflies.

Meanwhile, in the United States, the widespread use of pesticides, genetically modified crops, and large monoculture farms are drastically reducing the amount of plants that monarchs depend on, such as milkweed (*Asclepias*)—the plant on which monarchs lay their eggs and the caterpillars eat. Milkweed is often removed by farmers in the United States and Canada who view the plant as a pest or weed.

Government leaders sounded the alarm bells. In 2015 US president Barack Obama met with Mexican president Enrique Peña Nieto and Canadian prime minister Stephen Harper during a North American summit. Out of the meeting came the Pollinator Partnership Action Plan. It outlined continent-wide efforts to promote and protect pollinator health through research, habitat creation, and education. The United States, Mexico, and Canada would work together to implement transboundary conservation projects to protect the monarch and other important pollinators.

The plan called for collaboration among government agencies, private landowners, tribal communities, and NGOs to protect and rebuild pollinator habitats. At the center of the effort is the Monarch Joint Venture, a multistate collaborative of dozens of government agencies, NGOs, and private businesses to protect what's become known as the Monarch Highway. This critical migration corridor traces the middle part of the United States, from Texas north through the Dakotas and into Canada. The Monarch Joint Venture is focused on large-scale habitat restoration and protection across the region, as well as education and community engagement at the local level. The Monarch Joint Venture takes a leading role in organizing interstate efforts to restore milkweed and pollinator habitats along the more than 1,500 miles (2,414 km) of roadway in the monarch's migration route.

Mexican authorities have also increased protections to the monarch's critical wintering habitats. The Monarch Butterfly Biosphere Reserve is nestled high in forested mountains about 60 miles (100 km) west of Mexico City. The reserve is home to more than 138,000 acres (565 sq. km) of protected *oyamel* forests where monarch overwinter. The Mexican government has increased efforts to reduce illegal deforestation in the area. Leaders ramped up efforts to work with local farming communities on more responsible land practices to better protect the area around the reserve. However, due to poachers and other illegal businesses, even these protected areas are not entirely safe. In 2020 two activists involved in Mexico's monarch conservation efforts were killed just weeks apart. Authorities believe they ran afoul of illegal logging operations near the reserve.

ECOTOURISM

Another factor helping to protect the monarch's winter home in Mexico is a rise in ecotourism, low-impact tourism that brings visitors into natural environments. If done responsibly, ecotourism can benefit local communities as well as wildlife and their habitats. Ecotourism brings visitors into rural and small communities for low-impact activities such as hiking, bird-watching, river rafting, or snorkeling. These activities can help educate visitors and raise awareness of environmental threats to an area. Admission fees to a park or a permit fee for a rafting trip can go directly back to conservation efforts. Visitors will also spend money on hotels, restaurants, guides, and supplies, creating an entire eco-based economy with jobs and income for local people.

Nestled among the Cockscomb Mountains is the Cockscomb Basin Wildlife Sanctuary. Visitors often arrive with the hopes of spotting a jaguar, but are far more likely to simply see traces of one, such as footprints. However, visitors can hike through the rain forests and observe plenty of other wildlife, including monkeys, coatimundis, and over three hundred species of birds that call the reserve home.

One example of ecotourism is the Cockscomb Basin Wildlife Sanctuary in Belize. As the world's first sanctuary for jaguars, Cockscomb encompasses

THE DOWNSIDE OF ECOTOURISM

Ecotourism is not without its faults. Ecotourism industries that are not responsibly planned and managed can have serious negative effects on local communities and the natural environment—the two things ecotourism is supposed to help in the first place. Development can displace local peoples, where expensive hotels or restaurants replace affordable housing. Large companies that provide services, such as guides, can move in and outcompete smaller companies, forcing locals out of their livelihood. Sometimes, companies benefit from an ecotourism area, but very little of the profits is returned to the community to help protect the attractions. Ecotourism can also lead to an increase of visitors to exotic and remote areas. When poorly managed, increased foot traffic and other human activities can have devastating effects on these fragile environments.

Areas that rely on ecotourism dollars are often found in multiuse landscapes where many different communities have lived on and worked the lands for generations. For example, each year tourists from around the world flock to major national parks in Kenya and Tanzania to view and photograph famed African wildlife like elephants, zebras, and lions. Traditional communities, such as the Maasai people, still rely on traditional cattle ranching and small, subsistence farming on these lands. Protecting areas strictly for wildlife—and the tourist dollars they generate—can force smaller communities off their lands or restrict certain traditional land uses like hunting or cattle grazing. Sometimes, these management decisions are made by governing bodies that might not have the best interest of all communities in mind. Truly successful ecotourism requires giving people agency—the empowerment to be a part of decision-making and to have a voice in deciding what is good for their community, environment, and economy.

150 square miles (390 sq. km) of semitropical rain forest for the population of big cats to roam. This preserve also protects habitats for other unique wildlife as well as the forests and waterways in south-central Belize. Thousands of ecotourists from around the world come to Cockscomb to catch a glimpse of the elusive big cat. They also come to eat in local restaurants, hire a hiking guide, or perhaps pay for a rafting trip. Thanks to ecotourism, communities near the sanctuary have an economic incentive to protect the area and its population of big cats and other wildlife.

CHAPTER 8

THINK BIG, THINK LOCAL

The ideas of important figures in biology—
Mendel, Darwin, MacArthur, and Wilson—
helped us understand the processes and patterns of
life on Earth. We started to see how species change
over time and space. We are only beginning to
understand the human influence on our natural
environment and the long-term effects of habitat
fragmentation on worldwide biodiversity. Writer
David Quammen described it as "the world is in
pieces," a steady *drip, drip, drip*, as piece by piece
we fragment our Earth. With roads, cities, fences,
and border walls, we divide our landscapes into
smaller and smaller pieces. Eventually, animals like
the jaguar will have nowhere else to run, hemmed
in on all sides by humans. Isolated population
islands will remain in reserves and national parks,
but what are these but merely zoos without walls,
bars, and glass?

Extinction, of course, is a natural part of life. Evolution through natural selection ensures that extinctions will always occur. Some species will survive, and other species will die off. What's different is the *rate* at which extinction is occurring. Since the dawn of life on Earth, five mass extinctions have occurred. These extinctions claimed the dinosaurs. They claimed the giant mammals from the Pleistocene too. Many scientists believe that we are living through a sixth mass extinction. This mass extinction is our own doing. Some believe this new sixth extinction is occurring one thousand times faster than the natural rate of extinction.

We can protect our most vulnerable wildlife species. We've done it before. The black-footed ferret (*Mustela nigripes*), the American buffalo (*Bison bison*), and California condor (*Gymnogyps californianus*) are just a few examples of species that humans saved from the brink of extinction during the last century. Thanks to the tireless efforts of individuals, organizations, and governments, widespread collaborative efforts saved these endangered species.

CASE STUDY: AMPHIBIANS ON THE MOVE

The threats to biodiversity are not limited to exotic and far-off landscapes and animals. These threats are also not limited to large, wide-ranging animals like the pronghorn and jaguar. The effects of a changing world are also found in smaller scales, sometimes right in our own backyards.

Each spring when the snows have melted away in the deciduous (leaf-shedding) forests in the American Northeast, life slowly emerges from its long winter slumber. The melting snow and the first rains collect in depressions in the forest floor, creating ponds and pools that will soon explode with life. Each night in early spring, these tiny bodies of water come alive with the loud chorus of frogs and toads.

These vernal pools, small and temporary bodies of water, are found in deciduous forests during spring and early summer. Vernal pools are a lifeline for forest amphibians such as frogs, toads, salamanders, and newts. Unlike reptile or bird eggs, amphibian eggs require water to stay alive. Vernal pools act as a nursery and play a critical role in the earliest stages of an amphibian's life cycle. They are watery habitats providing food and shelter. And since they are temporary, vernal pools are also free of fish and other aquatic predators that might feed on the eggs or young amphibians.

Most species of amphibians spend the winter underground, hibernating during the cold winter months. But with the first signs of spring, the frogs, salamanders, and other amphibians emerge from their winter burrows. It's mating season for species such as the wood frog (*Rana sylvatica*) and spotted salamander (*Ambystoma maculatum*). With the first spring rains these tiny forest dwellers migrate to the vernal pool breeding grounds.

These migrations might be just a few hundred feet. But to the frog and the salamander, it can be a very dangerous journey. In many forests, the migration routes to the vernal pools cross roads and driveways. During peak migrations, when hundreds or thousands of amphibians make the journey in one night, wet roadways can be littered with crawling and hopping creatures desperately trying to reach the safety of the vernal pool. These migration corridors can turn into death traps.

Amphibians such as this wood frog rely on particular environmental conditions to survive. As climate change drastically shifts temperatures and weather patterns around the globe, amphibian populations are suffering tremendously. Programs like the Amphibian Migrations and Road Crossing Project can help protect amphibian species.

CITIZEN SCIENCE

Citizen science is a collaboration between scientists and volunteers. These projects greatly expand science's ability to collect data about a certain topic. Citizen science projects are becoming increasingly popular as this crowd-source method of data collection continues to contribute to the world of science. Citizen scientists are working on all kinds of projects, from backyard birds to bats and air quality to archaeology. There's something for everyone.

In the forests of upstate New York, the Amphibian Migrations and Road Crossing Project is working to protect these migration corridors. The project is a collaboration between the New York State Department of Environmental Conservation (NYSDEC) and Cornell University, a leader in citizen science programs. Citizen science projects invite nonscientists to work on research and conservation projects in many ways.

In the amphibian migration project, citizen scientists help collect valuable data. These volunteers are trained to identify amphibian species to record migration data. This valuable information can tell scientists about local species and their migration habits. These data can also tell scientists about local amphibian population trends by the number and diversity of amphibians detected year to year.

"Many individuals never have the opportunity to see how science can inform decision-making," says Laura Heady, project leader and a biologist for NYSDEC. "By being involved with citizen science, volunteers can learn while also contributing to the greater understanding . . . by gathering data or sharing their own observations."

Perhaps most important, citizen scientists help identify areas of amphibian migration and where these woodland creatures might need a little assistance crossing roadways on their way to the local pool. The project's citizen scientists work as "crossing guards" during the spring season. Wearing rain gear, headlamps, and safety vests, these volunteers work with local authorities to close or slow road traffic during big migrations. In the ten years since the project began, citizen science volunteers have helped more than nine thousand amphibians cross roadways safely.

Small, local efforts like these can have enormous impacts. For sensitive frogs, salamanders, and other amphibians, habitat fragmentation is a serious threat to long-term survival. According to the United States Geological Survey, nearly 50 percent of amphibian species in the Northeast are listed as threatened or endangered at the state or federal level. This is mostly because vernal pools are not protected habitats. These aquatic nurseries are vanishing as humans develop and fragment woodland landscapes.

It's not just a local problem either. Worldwide amphibian species are plummeting. Because the amphibian life cycle is so dependent on clean water, they are very vulnerable to the effects of water pollution. Runoff from pesticides and other chemicals used in our lawns or in farmlands drains into these pools, sometimes poisoning the water these animals depend on. Climate change and warming temperatures are also having devastating effects on amphibians, which rely on cool, wet habitats to survive.

A BRIGHT FUTURE . . . IF WE WANT IT

Our world is changing. Thanks to climate change, temperatures around the globe are getting warmer. Sea levels are rising, and destructive storms such as hurricanes and typhoons grow fiercer. And still we demand more from our planet as corporations and industries continue to clear forests for farmland and mine mountains for precious resources, as developers build houses on what used to be wilderness for a growing human population, and as governments approve environmentally destructive practices and projects for short-term economic gains.

The study of wildlife corridors—and how we can protect them—is a relatively new science. We are only beginning to understand how and why plants and animals move across the landscape as well as how important these corridors are for healthy populations of plants and animals. But people are starting to notice. Even Washington, DC, and state capitals are getting involved.

In 2019 the US House of Representatives introduced the Wildlife Corridors Conservation Act, which would provide "the conservation and restoration of habitats that facilitate the movement of native species that may be at risk due to habitat loss or fragmentation." The new law would protect wildlife corridors on federal public lands while also providing funding for states, tribes, and other organizations to protect corridors on nonfederal lands. It would also be a bottom-up approach to conservation, where government agencies and the public work with NGOs to identify wildlife corridors. In July 2020, the House of Representatives passed the Moving Forward Act, a law that would have funded major improvements to roads and railways across the nation. The act would have set aside $75 million for states to improve wildlife crossings and find other measures to reduce wildlife-vehicle collisions. More than a dozen states, from Florida to Oregon, continue to pursue and improve legislation to make wildlife crossings safer along their roadways.

These recent actions by the highest forms of government to protect wildlife corridors are a long time coming. It has begun to happen because of years of hard work from a multitude of sources. Scientists, researchers, wildlife agencies, and NGOs worked together to better understand the problem of habitat fragmentation and the importance of wildlife corridors. Educators, citizen scientists, and the concerned public—from hunters to hikers—helped raise awareness of habitat fragmentation and the corridors needed to keep these landscapes connected.

But this work is not limited to state capitals and Washington, DC.

By joining the fight against climate change and wildlife fragmentation, you can help literally change the landscape for future generations of people and wildlife alike.

Students around the world are standing up to protect the planet and demand their voices be heard. In March 2019, students from New York to Berlin, Germany, to Sidney, Australia, walked out of their schools to protest inaction on climate change. Meanwhile, the landmark case *Juliana v. United States* wound its way toward some of the highest courts in the nation. The lawsuit argued that a healthy and safe climate is a constitutional right and the US government has violated their duties by allowing activities that contribute to climate change. More and more, young people around the world are standing up to have their voices heard about the world they will soon inherit.

If the jaguar is going to make it in the United States, it will likely have to do it on its own. Reintroduction efforts are mostly impractical when it comes to large predators. Politics and pushback are far too fierce for such endeavors. If the jaguar wants to be in the United States, the big cat will find a way—as long as we give it a chance. Keeping the landscape connected, protecting core habitats and the corridors that connect them, and breaking down barriers that impeded movements is all the jaguar needs to reestablish its range here in the US.

So what happens if the jaguar vanishes from the Borderlands? The desert ecosystems of the Sky Islands won't collapse. There won't be any drastic changes if the jaguar never steps foot in the United States again. Large predators, by nature, are rare. There's just not that many of them on Earth. The jaguar is no exception. But what do we lose if we lose the jaguar? To answer that, we can ask what we lost when we lost the passenger pigeon, the dodo, or the Tasmanian tiger. With the extinction of more and more species, we lose part of our heritage. We

WHAT CAN YOU DO TO MAKE A DIFFERENCE?

Scientists and conservationists aren't the only people helping to protect wild creatures and wild places. Thanks, in part to the internet, there are more ways to help than ever. Here are just a few things you can do to make a difference in your community and beyond:

- Money talks. Do your research to know about the food and products you and your family purchase. Are they made from eco-friendly materials? Is the food grown or caught in a sustainable manner? How we spend our money is perhaps our most powerful conservation tool.
- Get inside, and get outside. Visit zoos, aquariums, botanical gardens, wildlife reserves, and state and national parks. The money you spend visiting these places will help support scientific research or wildlife conservation.
- Get in the game. Check out a citizen science project in your area. Go to iNaturalist (https://www.inaturalist.org) and Citizenscience.gov to learn about citizen science projects near you.

lose another magnificent species that traveled millions of years to get to this point, to coexist with us in a shared landscape, another species that survived when countless others went extinct.

Through dedication, smart science, and international collaboration, conservationists may be able to bring the jaguar back to the United States—for good.

- Get dirty. Plant native vegetation at your home or school. Even the smallest patch of green provides habitat and corridors for plants and animals of all sizes.
- Get pretty. Native wildflower gardens not only provide dazzling flowers to enjoy, but they'll also provide vital resources for an array of pollinators like butterflies, bees, and hummingbirds.
- Provide shelter. Installing houses for birds or bats is a great way to offer shelter to some local winged friends. Do some research to learn what species can be found in your area and what kind of shelter they require.
- Get involved. Join a wildlife conservation organization. Donate your time or money to a local organization that's protecting wildlife and habitat in your area. It's a great way to stay informed.
- Speak up! Your voice matters. Want to fight climate change? Start a club at school. Want to help protect the open spaces where you live? Write to your local representative. Want to help jaguars, pronghorn, or butterflies? Helping our wild friends begins with YOU.

GLOSSARY

ALGORITHM: a set of rules for solving a problem, usually performed by a computer

BIODIVERSITY: the variety of life in the world, an ecosystem, or a habitat

BIOGEOGRAPHY: a branch of biology that deals with the geographic distribution of plants and animals

CARRYING CAPACITY: the number of individuals that an ecosystem can support

CITIZEN SCIENCE: the collection of data by the general public as part of a project administered by professional scientists

CONNECTIVITY: a measure to the extent that parcels of land are connected

DEOXYRIBONUCLEIC ACID (DNA): a molecule that carries genetic information of cells that define growth, development, and function

DISPERSE: to spread over a wide area; to move away from the place where one originates or was born

EMPIRICAL DATA: information gathered through observation and experimentation

EPOCH: an extended period characterized by certain developments

EXTIRPATED: locally extinct

FLAGSHIP SPECIES: a unique or charismatic species chosen to represent a conservation effort

GAME BIRD: a bird hunted for sport or food

GROUND-TRUTHING: act of verifying data

HABITAT FRAGMENTATION: habitat loss that divides habitats into smaller, disconnected pieces

HEREDITY: passing of physical or mental characteristics from parents to offspring

HERITAGE: features belonging to a certain culture or society

IMMIGRATION: travel to another area or country to permanently live there

IMPERILED: at risk or being harmed

INBREEDING: breeding between closely related individuals, especially over multiple generations

LANDSCAPE ECOLOGY: the study of relations between ecological processes and the physical environment

LINEAGE: line of descent from an ancestor

MELANISTIC: dark coloration of fur, skin, or feathers; an inherited trait

MICROBE: a very small organism, typically only seen using a microscope

MIGRATION: seasonal movement of animals from one place to another

MONOCULTURE: growing a single crop in an area

MORAL: the principal of right and wrong

NICHE: the function or role of a species within an ecosystem

OSSIFIED: turn into bone

POPULATION: a group of individuals of the same species living together

RANGE: a geographical area where a species can be found

REGULATED: control or supervise something by using laws and rules

RESILIENT: able to recover or survive from difficult situations

SCAT: the droppings of an animal

SPECIES RICHNESS: the number of species living within an area

SUBSPECIES: a population of a species geographically or genetically distinct from other populations of that species

TEMPERATE: a climate with moderate temperatures and seasonal changes

TERRITORY: an area that an individual claims and will defend

TRANSBOUNDARY: crossing international boundaries and borders

TRANSLOCATED: transport an individual from one place to another

UMBRELLA SPECIES: conservation concept whereby protecting one species will also protect a number of other species

VERNAL POOL: temporary pools or bodies of water that provide habitat for certain animals and plants

SOURCE NOTES

54   Charles Darwin, *On the Origin of Species by Means of Natural Section, or Preservation of Favoured Races in the Struggle for Life* (New York: W. W. Norton, 2006), 78.

66–67   Juan Carlos Bravo, personal interview, January 12, 2018.

67–68   Bravo.

68   Bravo.

76   Miguel Gómez, personal interview, May 4, 2018.

77   Gómez.

79   Gómez.

91–92   Diana Friedeberg, personal interview with the author, April 20, 2018.

93   Friedeberg, personal interview with the author, May 1, 2018.

95–96   Friedeberg.

105   David Quammen and Kris Ellingsen, *The Song of the Dodo: Island Biogeography in an Age of Extinctions* (New York: Scribner, 1996), 549.

108   Laura Heady, personal interview with the author, May 2018.

110   Wildlife Corridors Conservation Act of 2018, H.R. 7232, 115th Congress, https://congress.gov/bill/115th-congress/house-bill/7232/.

SELECTED BIBLIOGRAPHY

Ament, R., R. Callahan, M. McClure, M. Reuling, and G. Tabor. *Wildlife Connectivity: Fundamentals for Conservation Action*. Bozeman, MT: Center for Large Landscape Conservation, 2014.

Associated Press. "Students Name Arizona Wild Jaguar 'El Jefe.'" *AZ Central*, November 3, 2015. https://amp.azcentral.com/amp/75100458.

"The Beginnings of the National Wilderness Preservation System." Wilderness Connect, University of Montana. Accessed May 14, 2018. https://www.wilderness .net/nwps/fastfacts.

Bravo, Juan Carlos. "Conservacion with Two C's, Part 1." *The Wildlands Network Blog*. Accessed February 2, 2018. https://wildlandsnetwork.org/blog/conservacion -with-two-cs-1/.

Bravo, Juan Carlos, and Katie Davis. *Four Species on the Brink: And the Wall That Would Push Them toward Extinction*. Seattle: Wildlands Network, 2017.

Brower, Lincoln P., and Robert M. Pyle. "The Interchange of Migratory Monarchs between Mexico and the Western United States, and the Importance of Floral Corridors to the Fall and Spring Migrations." In *Conserving Migratory Pollinators and Nectar Corridors in Western North America*. Edited by Gary Paul Nabhan, 114–160. Tucson: University of Arizona Press, 2004.

Brown, David E., and Carlos A. López González. *Borderland Jaguars (Tigres de la Frontera)*. Salt Lake City: University of Utah Press, 2001.

Bruilliard, Karin. "The Grizzlies Are Coming." *Washington Post*. Accessed March 10, 2018. https://www.washingtonpost.com/graphics/2017/national/environment/grizzly -bear-population-spreads/.

Calderón, Roberto Solís, Blanca Xiomara Mora Alvarez, Jaime Lobato Reyes, Eligio García Serrano, and Héctor Silva Rodríguez. "The Monarch Butterfly Biosphere Reserve, Michoacan, Mexico." In *Conserving Migratory Pollinators and Nectar Corridors in Western North America*. Edited by Gary Paul Nabhan, 167–177. Tucson: University of Arizona Press, 2004.

Chung, Emily. "Banff Bears Use Trans-Canada Highway Crossings to Find Mates." CBC, February 14, 2014. http://www.cbc.ca/news/technology/banff-bears-use-trans -canada-wildlife-crossings-to-find-mates-1.2542362.

Coalition for Sonoran Desert Protection. "Three Wildlife Crossings Funded for Oracle Road." *Coalition Newsletter*, no. 39 (Summer 2010). Accessed March 18, 2018. https://www.sonorandesert.org/uploads/files/FOD_39_FINAL_240.pdf.

Darwin, Charles. *On the Origin of Species by Means of Natural Section, or Preservation of Favoured Races in the Struggle for Life.* First published 1859 by John Murray (London). New York: W. W. Norton, 2006.

"Florida Panther Population Estimate Update." United States Fish and Wildlife Service. Accessed November 26, 2017. https://www.fws.gov/southeast/news/2017/02/florida-panther-population-estimate-updated/.

Frej, Willa. "How US Immigration Policy Has Changed Since 9/11." Huffington Post, September 9, 2016. https://www.huffingtonpost.com/entry/us-immigration-since-911_us_57d05479e4b0a48094a71bc0.

Gibbens, Sarah. "Nearly 150,000 Bornean Orangutans Lost Since 1999, Cutting Population in Half." *National Geographic*, February 15, 2018. https://news.nationalgeographic.com/2018/02/orangutan-habitat-loss-hunting-killing-borneo-spd/.

Guynup, Sharon. "The Jaguar Freeway." *Smithsonian Magazine*, October 2011. https://www.smithsonianmag.com/science-nature/the-jaguar-freeway-73586097/.

Hannibal, Mary Ellen. *The Spine of the Continent: The Race to Save America's Last, Best Wilderness.* Guilford, CT: Lyons, 2016.

Hast, M. H. "The Larynx of Roaring and Non-Roaring Cats." *Journal of Anatomy* 163 (1989): 117–121.

Hilty, Jodi A., William Z. Lidicker Jr., and Adina M. Merenlender. *Corridor Ecology: The Science and Practice of Linking Landscapes for Biodiversity Conservation.* Washington, DC: Island, 2006.

Hornocker, Maurice, and Sharon Negri. *Cougar: Ecology and Conservation.* Chicago: University of Chicago Press, 2009.

Karpilow, Quentin, Ilana Solomon, Alejandro Villamar Calderón, Manuel Pérez-Rocha, and Stuart Trew. *TODAY: NAFTA: 20 Years of Costs to Communities and the Environment.* Oakland: Sierra Club, March 2014. https://content.sierraclub.org/www/press-releases/2013/10/today-nafta-20-years-costs-communities-environment.

Lasky, Jesse R., Walter Jetz, and Timothy H. Keitt. "Conservation Biogeography of the US-Mexico Border: A Transcontinental Risk Assessment of Barriers to Animal Dispersal." *Diversity and Distributions* 17 (2011): 673–687.

López-Hoffman, Laura, Emily D. McGovern, Robert G. Varady, and Karl W. Flessa, eds. *Conservation of Shared Environments.* Tucson: University of Arizona Press, 2009.

MacArthur, Robert H., and Edward O. Wilson. *The Theory of Island Biogeography.* Princeton, NJ: Princeton University Press, 1967.

Macdonald, David W., Andrew J. Loveridge, and Alan Rabinowitz. "Felid Future:

Crossing Disciplines, Borders, and Generations." In *Biology and Conservation of Wild Felids*. Edited by D. W. Macdonald and A. J. Loveridge. Oxford: Oxford University Press, 2010.

Mahler, Richard. *In the Jaguar's Shadow*. New Haven, CT: Yale University Press, 2009.

———. "The Tenuous Fate of the Southwest's Last Jaguars." *High Country News*, May 30, 2016. https://www.northernjaguarproject.org/the-tenuous-fate-of-the -southwests-last-jaguars.

Marinelli, Janet. "Can the Monarch Highway Save a Butterfly Under Siege?" Yale Environment 360 (July 11, 2017). https://e360.yale.edu/features/can-the-monarch -highway-help-save-a-butterfly-under-siege.

Mark, Jason. "How Trump's Border Wall Could Block the Most Exciting Wildlife Comeback in North America." Oakland: *Sierra*, August 22, 2017. https://www .sierraclub.org/sierra/2017-5-september-october/feature/how-trumps-border-wall -could-block-most-exciting-wildlife.

Matthew, Sean M., Jon P. Beckmann, and Amanda R. Hardy. "Recommendations of Road Passage Design for Jaguars." Wildlife Conservation Society, final report to the US Fish and Wildlife Service in response to Solicitation F14PX00340, submitted January 23, 2015 (updated September 22, 2015), 31.

McLellan, Bruce N., and Frederick W. Hovey. "Natal Dispersal of Grizzly Bears." *Canadian Journal of Zoology* 79, no. 5 (May 2001): 838–844.

McRae, Brad H., Brett G. Dickson, Timothy H. Keitt, and Viral B. Shah. "Using Circuit Theory to Model Connectivity in Ecology, Evolution, and Conservation." *Ecology* 89, no. 10 (October 2008). https://esajournals.onlinelibrary.wiley.com/doi /abs/10.1890/07-1861.1.

Miller, T. Christian, Kiah Collier, and Julián Aguilar. "The Taking: How the Federal Government Abused Its Power to Seize Property for a Border Fence." Texas Tribune, December 14, 2017. https://www.texastribune.org/2017/12/14/border-land-grab -government-abused-power-seize-property-fence/.

Morin, Peter J. *Community Ecology*. Malden, MA: Blackwell, 1999.

"Northeast Amphibian Research and Monitoring Initiative." United States Geological Survey. Accessed April 14, 2018. https://www.usgs.gov/centers/pwrc/science /northeast-amphibian-research-and-monitoring-initiative?qt-science_center _objects=0#qt-science_center_objects/.

Nowicki, Dan. "Senator John McCain Aims to Revive Immigration Reform When He Returns to Congress." *AZ Central*, August 3, 2017. http://www.azcentral.com /story/news/politics/arizona/2017/08/03/senator-john-mccain-aims-revive -immigration-reform-when-he-returns-congress/537758001/.

O'Brien, J. S., and W. E. Johnson. "The Evolution of Cats." *Scientific American*, July 2007, 68–75.

Onorato, Dave, Chris Belden, Mark Cunningham, Darrell Land, Roy McBride, and Melody Roelke. "Long-Term Research on the Florida Panther (*Puma concolor coryi*): Historical Findings and Future Obstacles to Population Persistence." In *Biology and Conservation of Wild Felids*. Edited by D. W. Macdonald and A. J. Loveridge. Oxford: Oxford University Press, 2010.

"Oracle Road Cameras Capture More Than Wildlife Using New Crossings." *Arizona Daily Star*. Accessed March 2, 2018. http://tucson.com/news/local/oracle-road -cameras-capture-more-than-wildlife-using-newcrossings/article_66a1ae5a-09ac-11e7 -adfe-2fa8456a516e.html.

Pimm, Stuart L., H. Lee Jones, and Jared Diamond. "On the Risk of Extinction." *American Natural History* 132 (December 1988): 757–785.

Powledge, Fred. "Island Biogeography's Lasting Impact." *BioScience* 53, no. 11 (November 2003), 1032–1038. https://academic.oup.com/bioscience/article/53/11 /1032/259831.

Reichard, Sean. "Research Chart Routes to Grizzly Reunion." Yellowstone Insider, December 5, 2017. https://yellowstoneinsider.com/2017/12/05/researchers-chart -routes-grizzly-reunion.

Rodríquez-Soto, Clarita, Octavio Monroy-Vilchis, and Martha M. Zarco-Gonzalez. "Corridors for Jaguar (*Panthera onca*) in Mexico: Conservation Strategies." *Journal for Nature Conservation* 21 (December 2013): 438–443.

Rosas-Rosas, Octavio C., Louis C. Bender, and Raul Valdez. "Jaguar and Puma Predation on Cattle Calves in Northeastern Sonora, Mexico." *Rangeland Ecology and Management* 61 (September 2008): 554–560.

Schafer, Craig L. "Land Use Planning: A Potential Force for Retaining Habitat Connectivity in the Greater Yellowstone Ecosystem and Beyond." *Global Ecology and Conservation* 3 (January 2015): 256–278.

Siciliano, John. "DHS Waives More Than 30 Environmental Laws to Speed Trump's Border Wall." *Washington Examiner*, January 22, 2018. http://www .washingtonexaminer.com/dhs-waives-more-than-30-environmental-laws -to-speed-trumps-border-wall/article/2646731.

Solomon, Eldra, Linda Berg, and Diana W. Martin. *Biology*. 8th ed. Belmont, CA: Thomson Brooks/Cole, 2008.

Soulé, Michael E., Allison C. Alberts, and Douglas T. Bolger. "The Effects of Habitat Fragmentation of Chaparral Plants and Vertebrates." *Oikos* 63 (February 1992): 39–47.

Soulé, Michael E., and Daniel Simberloff. "What Do Genetics and Ecology Tell Us about the Design of Nature Reserves?" *Biological Conservation*, 1986, 19–40.

Town of Cortlandt, NY. "DEC Announces Start of Annual Frog and Salamander Migration." News release, April 14, 2018. http://www.townofcortlandt.com/cn/news /index.cfm?NID=46217&jump2=0.

United States Fish and Wildlife Service. *Draft Recovery Plan for the Sonoran Pronghorn (*Antilocapra Americana sonoriensis*), Second Revision*. Albuquerque: USFWS, 2015.

Vasilijević, Maja, Kevan Zunckel, Matthew McKinney, Boris Erg, Michael Schoon, Tatjana Rosen Michel, Craig Groves, and Adrian Phillips. "Transboundary Conservation: A Systematic and Integrated Approach." *Best Practice Protected Area Guidelines Series*, no. 23 (May 2015). https://www.academia.edu/12527121 /Transboundary_Conservation_a_systematic_and_integrated_approach/.

Wagner, Stephen C. "Keystone Species." *Nature Education Knowledge* 3, no. 10 (2010): 51. https://www.nature.com/scitable/knowledge/library/keystone-species-15786127.

Wallace, Alfred Russel. *Island Life*. New York: Prometheus Books, 1998.

Weber, William, and Alan Rabinowitz. "A Global Perspective on Large Carnivore Conservation." *Conservation Biology* 10, no. 4 (August 1996): 1046–1054.

Weisbrot, Mark, Stephan Lefebvre, and Joseph Sammut. *Did NAFTA Help Mexico? An Assessment after 20 Years*. Washington, DC: Center for Economic and Policy Research, 2014.

"Which Everyday Products Contain Palm Oil?" World Wildlife Fund. Accessed April 28, 2018. https://www.worldwildlife.org/pages/which-everyday-products-contain -palm-oil.

Wilson, E. O. *The Diversity of Life*. New York: W. W. Norton, 1999.

Zimmer, Carl. *Evolution: The Triumph of an Idea*. New York: Harper Collins, 2001.

FURTHER INFORMATION

BOOKS

Childs, Jack, and Mary Ann Childs. *Ambushed on the Jaguar Trail*. Tucson: Rio Nuevo, 2008.
  Borderlands ranchers, the authors used camera traps to document the diversity of wildlife along the US-Mexico border. Spellbinding images of animals in the natural environments populate this book.

Downer, Ann. *The Animal Mating Game: The Wacky, Weird World of Sex in the Animal Kingdom*. Minneapolis: Twenty-First Century Books, 2017.
  This fun, informative, and visually engaging book explores the wide world of animal reproduction. Learn about the life cycles, courting, and mating habits of a range of animals, from hyenas, bats, and penguins to spiders, frogs, and snakes.

———. *Wild Animal Neighbors: Sharing Our Urban World*. Minneapolis: Twenty-First Century Books, 2016.
  This colorful and fascinating book explores some of the conflicts and solutions for living in harmony with our wild neighbors as humans expand into their habitats.

Glenn, Warner. *Eyes of Fire: Encounter with a Borderlands Jaguar*. New York: Treasure Chest, 1996.
  The book tells about the afternoon in 1996 when hunter Warner Glenn stumbled upon a jaguar in the Peloncillo Mountains of Arizona. Glenn's stunning photographs of the day capture the excitement of a once-in-a-lifetime encounter that changed big cat conservation in the United States.

Hannibal, Mary Ellen. *The Spine of the Continent: The Race to Save America's Last, Best Wilderness*. Guilford, CT: Lyons, 2016.
  Hannibal explores biogeography and the people fighting to save the vital linkages for wildlife in the American West. The author meets with scientists working with grizzly bears, pronghorn antelope, and jaguars in northern Mexico.

Hirsch, Rebecca E. *De-Extinction: The Science of Bringing Lost Species Back to Life*. Minneapolis: Twenty-First Century Books, 2017.
  Learn about scientific efforts to reintroduce extinct animals, including woolly mammoths, passenger pigeons, bucardos, and dodo birds.

Quammen, David. *Song of the Dodo: Island Biogeography in the Age of Extinction*. New York: Scribner, 1997.
  With brilliant storytelling, writer and adventurer David Quammen travels the world exploring how island biogeography is pushing many species to the very edge of extinction.

Rabinowitz, Alan. *Jaguar: One Man's Struggle to Establish the World's First Jaguar Preserve*. Washington, DC: Island, 2000.
  Part memoir, part science adventure, this book explores Rabinowitz's journey to study jaguars in Belize, efforts that ultimately resulted in the world's first jaguar preserve.

Schyler, Krista. *Continental Divide: Wildlife, People, and the Border Wall.* College Station: Texas A&M University Press, 2012.
   Using stunning photos and writing, Schyler explores the effects of the border wall on the unique wildlife, habitats, and people of the border region.

FILMS

In Search of the Jaguar. Directed by Kate Churchill. Los Angeles: 20th Century Fox, 2006.
   Narrated by Glenn Close, this National Geographic documentary follows Alan Rabinowitz and others and their quest to protect the habitats and corridors big cats need to survive in the Americas.

Nature: Big Cats. Chicago: Questar Entertainment, 2005.
   In this two-part series from PBS *Nature*, the first disc is "Jaguar: Year of the Cat," which follows jaguars in the rain forests of Belize. Disc 2, "Chasing Big Cats," follows several species of big cats in Africa.

VIDEOS

E. O. Wilson, Of Ants and Men
   http://www.pbs.org/program/eo-wilson/
   This two-hour PBS special celebrates the life and work of scientist E. O. Wilson and how his ideas changed how we view the world. The special focuses on his work with Robert MacArthur and their book *The Theory of Island Biogeography*.

"The Wall"
   https://www.usatoday.com/border-wall/documentaries/105143752
   A series of short web videos produced by USA Today captures the many complex issues surrounding the border wall, from endangered species protection to drug trafficking and human migration.

"Wildlife and the Wall"
   https://www.youtube.com/watch?v=smeoiCqS_YU
   In this short web video, filmmaker Ben Masters travels the Rio Grande in Texas to explore the impacts of the border wall on wildlife.

WEBSITES

Coalition for Sonoran Desert Protection
   https://www.sonorandesert.org
   The coalition has brought together more than two dozen organizations to collaborate on projects to protect wildlife and their habitats in the Sonoran Desert of Arizona and Mexico.

iNaturalist Citizen Science
   https://www.inaturalist.org
   This database of citizen science projects lets you find exciting science projects near where you live.

International Union for the Conservation of Nature (IUCN) Red List
http://www.iucnredlist.org
This authoritative database includes the endangerment status of many of the
world's species.

Journey of the Jaguar
https://www.journeyofthejaguar.org
Follow the Panthera team as they work to save vital jaguar corridors from Mexico
to Brazil.

Monarch Joint Venture
https://monarchjointventure.org
Read the latest in monarch butterfly research, and learn how to get involved in
protecting monarch habitats.

National Geographic Big Cat Initiative
https://www.nationalgeographic.org/projects/big-cats-initiative/
Learn about National Geographic's work collaborating with organizations to
help save big cats around the world, from jaguars in Belize to African lions and
Asian tigers.

Northern Jaguar Project
https://www.northernjaguarproject.org
Learn about the Northern Jaguar Project to protect the jaguar's northernmost
populations in Mexico. View a database of stunning images of wildlife on the
reserve.

Panthera's Corridor Initiative
https://www.panthera.org/initiative/jaguar-corridor-initiative
Follow Alan Rabinowitz and Panthera's journey to protect the vital corridors for
jaguars in Central and South America.

Roundtable on Sustainable Palm Oil
https://www.rspo.org
The nonprofit organization works with the palm oil industry to develop
sustainable practices for wildlife and people alike.

Wildlands Network Borderlands Campaign
https://wildlandsnetwork.org/campaigns/borderlands/
Learn about the Wildlands Network's work to protect open spaces in the
Borderlands for jaguars, black bears, wolves, and pronghorn.

Wildlife Conservation Society: Big Cats
https://www.wcs.org/our-work/wildlife/big-cats
Based out of the Bronx Zoo in New York City, the Wildlife Conservation Society
has led groundbreaking work protecting jaguars and other big cats.

INDEX

ABOUT THE AUTHOR

Elizabeth Webb is a writer living in New Mexico, not far from where the Borderlands jaguars roam. She's spent much of her adult life exploring and photographing the plants and animals of the Desert Southwest. This is her first book for young people.

PHOTO ACKNOWLEDGMENTS

Image credits: Photos by the author. Additional images: JL Jahn/Shutterstock.com, p. 10; Laura Westlund/Independent Picture Service, pp. 13, 14–15, 38, 47, 49, 70, 90, nidpor/Alamy Stock Photo, p. 26; Library of Congress/Corbis/VCG/Getty Images, p. 31; Joe Raedle/Getty Images, p. 41; sunsinger/Shutterstock.com, pp. 52–53; World History Archive/Alamy Stock Photo, p. 55; Jim Harrison/Wikimedia Commons (2.5 Generic license), p. 59; PATSUDA PARAMEE/Shutterstock.com, pp. 104–105.

Cover: W. Drew Senter, Longleaf Photography/Moment/Getty Images.